Faith First

Grade One

Faith First Development Team

RCL⭑
Benziger

Allen, Texas

"The Ad Hoc Committee to Oversee
the Use of the Catechism,
National Conference of Catholic Bishops,
has found this catechetical series, copyright 2000,
to be in conformity with
the *Catechism of the Catholic Church*."

NIHIL OBSTAT
Rev. Msgr. Glenn D. Gardner, J.C.D.
Censor Librorum

IMPRIMATUR
† Most Rev. Charles V. Grahmann
Bishop of Dallas

February 16, 1999

The Nihil Obstat and Imprimatur are official declarations that
the material reviewed is free of doctrinal or moral error. No
implication is contained therein that those granting the Nihil
Obstat and Imprimatur agree with the contents, opinions, or
statements expressed.

Send all inquiries to:
RCL Benziger
206 East Bethany Drive
Allen, Texas 75002-3804

Toll Free   877-275-4725
Fax   800-688-8356

Visit us at **www.RCLBenziger.com**
          www.FaithFirst.com

Printed in the United States of America

20301   ISBN 978-0-7829-0913-5 (Student Book)
20311   ISBN 978-0-7829-0914-2 (Teacher Guide)
20321   ISBN 978-0-7829-0915-9 (Catechist Guide)

9th printing.
Manufactured for RCL Benziger in Madison, WI, USA.
August 2010.

ACKNOWLEDGMENTS

Excerpts from the *New American Bible with Revised New
Testament and Psalms* Copyright © 1991, 1986, 1970
Confraternity of Christian Doctrine, Inc., Washington, DC.
Used with permission. All rights reserved. No portion of the
New American Bible may be reprinted without permission in
writing from the copyright holder.

All adaptations of Scripture are based on the *New American
Bible with Revised New Testament and Psalms* Copyright
© 1991, 1986, 1970 Confraternity of Christian Doctrine, Inc.,
Washington, DC.

Excerpts from the English translation of *The Roman Missal*
© 1973, International Committee on English in the Liturgy,
Inc. (ICEL); excerpts from the English translation of *Rite of
Baptism for Children* © 1969, ICEL; excerpts from the English
translation of *A Book of Prayers* © 1982, ICEL; excerpts from
Book of Blessings © 1987, ICEL. All rights reserved.

Photograph and Art Credits appear on page 288.

Faith First Development Team

Developing a religion program requires the gifts
and talents of many different individuals working
together as a team. RCL Benziger is proud
to acknowledge these dedicated people.

Advisory Board

Rev. Louis J. Cameli
Judith Deckers
Rev. Robert D. Duggan
Rev. Virgil Elizondo
Jacquie Jambor
Maureen A. Kelly
Elaine McCarron, SCN
Rev. Frank McNulty
Rev. Ronald J. Nuzzi
Kate Sweeney Ristow

Grade 1 Writers

Student Book

Nancy M. DeStefano
Joanne McGinnis
Yvette Nelson
Margherita Rader

Catechist/Teacher Guides

Susan Jones
Yvette Nelson

Editorial

Blake Bergen
Patricia A. Classick
Ed DeStefano
Jack Gargiulo
Karen Griffith
Anne Battes Kirby
Keith Ksobiech
Ronald C. Lamping
Joan Lathen
Ed Leach
Eileen McGrath
Anna Dolores Ready
Myrtle E. Teffeau

Art and Design

Pat Bracken
Andrea Friedman
Kristy Howard
Sheila Lehnert
Karen Malzeke-McDonald
Margaret Matus
Carol-Anne Wilson

Production

Mark Burgdorff
Laura Fremder
Becky Ivey
Jenna Nelson

Executive Board

Maryann Nead   Kim Duty

Richard C. Leach

Contents

Unit 4—We Pray

We Celebrate

Welcome to Faith First

My name is _____.

I like to be called _____.

One of the best things about me is _____

_____.

This year I hope I learn _____.

_____

Here is a picture
of my family.

Favorite Things

Animal _____

Bible Story _____

Food _____

Holiday _____

Game _____

_____

A Prayer for the Beginning of First Grade

Dear God,

I am happy to be in first grade. I think it will be fun. There
will be many things to learn. Help me to learn how much
you love me. Help me to learn to show my love for you.

Amen.

Parent Page—Unit 1: We Believe

Your Role

This is a special year for your first graders and for your family. For many children this is their first experience with formal religious education. This may be a new experience for you as well. You have already taught your child about God and Jesus and something of our Catholic faith. In religious education classes your child will be taught in a more structured way about doctrine, about Scripture, and about our liturgical year. You are a partner in this process. You have a unique opportunity to relate what is being taught in class to what is happening at home. You help to connect faith to life for your child.

It is good for us as parents to remind ourselves, from time to time, that we are the models from which our children learn their value systems. If faith is important and practiced in your life, then chances are it will become important for your child as well. Children really do learn what they live.

What We're Teaching

The first unit teaches the children about the Creed. The children learn about the Bible and how it teaches us about God, our loving Father. They learn about Jesus who came to teach us about God's love for us and to show us how to live as children of God. They learn that the Holy Spirit is always with us to help us. They read the Scripture story of the Annunciation and the Good Samaritan. We encourage you to read your child's book. It will help you see exactly what your child is learning and help you to engage your child in conversation about what he or she is learning.

Visit our web site at www.FaithFirst.com

What Difference Does It Make?

As a first grader, your child will learn many new things and will grow in many ways this year. Growth in faith should be a very important part of this year for your child. As you share your faith with your child, he or she can see that these lessons are important to you and they will be important to him or her as well. Perhaps you can share a time when you have experienced God's love in your life. As you read through the lessons in your child's book, think of ways that you can help him or her see what difference this knowledge can make in your child's life. Adapt what is in the book to your child's life experiences. Help your child reflect on the people and events in his or her life and how God is part of those times. In this way you help your child learn lessons about God's love that can last a lifetime. That's the best possible way for your child to be taught.

Unit Opener Photographs: (top left) stained-glass window of Mary; (top right) cross from El Salvador; (bottom) father and children reading the Bible.

God Loves Us

We Pray

Lord God,
We believe
in you.
We hope in you.
We love you.
Amen.

God loves each one of us very much. God wants us to know and love him. What do you know about God?

We learn about God and show our love for God in many ways.

We Know God Loves Us

Faith Focus
Who helps you to know God?

Faith Words
pray
We pray when we listen and talk to God.

It is the first day of school! We meet new friends. We talk and listen to them. God is your friend in a very special way. This year you will learn more about God.

God knows us very well. He loves us all the time, and we love him with all our heart. God wants us to know and love him.

Our Families Help Us

Our families help us to know and love God. At home we learn to **pray.** Our families help us learn to talk and listen to God. Sometimes we pray together.

Our Church Helps Us

People in our Church know and
love God. They help us to know
and love God too. We hear stories
about people who show us ways to
love God. We help one another
and learn to pray together.

Learning About Love

Our families and Church help us to
learn ways to love God. Color the Xs in
one color and the Os in another color.
Find out who always loves us.

Faith Words

Bible
  The Bible is the written Word of God. It is the story of God's love for us.

Abraham
  Abraham was a great leader of God's people.

God loves and knows every person. God wants everyone to know him and love him too.

God Chooses a Leader

The **Bible** has many wonderful stories that tell us about God's love. Read this story about **Abraham** and Sarah.

Abraham and Sarah were friends of God. They lived a long time ago. They had no children. God chose Abraham to be a great leader. God said to Abraham, "I am giving you a promise. You will have many children. You will live on this land forever.

You will be the father of many nations. I will bless your wife Sarah. She will give birth to a son."

Based on Genesis 17:1–6

God loved Abraham and Sarah. God loves everyone.

With My Family

Ask a family member to read a story from the Bible. Share your favorite Bible stories together.

Sharing God's Love

Abraham and Sarah told everyone about God's love. Draw the people who tell you about God's love.

God loves us very much. God gave us a special gift to know him.

God's Special Gift

God gave us the gift of **Jesus.** Jesus is God's own Son, who came to live with us.

Jesus taught us about God. Jesus taught us over and over again how much God loves us.

Jesus told us that God is always with us. God is love.

What do you think of when you hear the name Jesus?

What Does This Mean to Me?

We learn about God's love for us in many ways.

God's Love

Draw a picture of the different ways you can learn about God's love.

Bible

Jesus

Family

Church

My Faith Choice

Check one way you will learn more about God.

_____ I will ask someone to read a Bible story to me.

_____ I will talk to God.

And now we pray. Guide me in your truth and teach me, for you are God.

Psalm 25:5

15

Chapter Review

Draw a line to connect the words with their meanings.

Words	Meanings
Bible	A time when we listen and talk to God
Jesus	The written Word of God
pray	God's Son, who became one of us

Use the words in the box to fill in the blanks.

God	Church	love

1. We learn about God through our
   C_____.

2. The Bible tells us about G_____.

3. Jesus told us about God's l_____ for us.

Think and share with your family.
Name two ways you and your family know that God loves you.

Visit our web site at www.FaithFirst.com

God Is Our Father and Our Creator

We Pray

Our Father
in heaven,
hallowed be
your name.
Amen.

The world is a
wonderful place.
The world is one
of God's gifts to
us. What does the
world tell us
about God?

*God gave us the
sun, the moon, and
the stars. Plants,
animals, water,
and people are all
God's gifts.*

God Our Father and Creator

Faith Focus

Why do we call God the Creator?

Faith Words

Creator
God is the Creator. God made everything that is good.

It is fun to make things. What do you like to make? God made things too. God made everything that is good!

God Our Creator

God made the whole world. God is the **Creator.** The Bible tells us that everything God created is good!

God looked at everything that he made. He saw that it was good.

Based on Genesis 1:31

God made everything because God is love. The world is full of the wonderful gifts created by God.

Drawing God's World

Everything God made is good. Think of your favorite part of God's creation. Draw it in the picture of the world.

Faith Focus

Why are people the most special part of creation?

Faith Words

people

People are God's creation. God created people in his image and likeness.

A Special Gift

The Bible tells us that God created everything. First God made the world. Then God created people. People are the most special part of creation. The first part of the Bible tells us this story.

God made people. People were created in God's image. God put them in charge of everything he had made. God blessed them. God gave them the world to care for. God looked at everything he had made and saw that it was very good. Then God rested from the work of creation.

Based on Genesis 1:26–31, 2:1–2

God is the Creator of all **people.** We are very special to God. We are very good. We are created in God's image and likeness.

God Made Me

God created you. You are special! Draw a picture of yourself. Then write your name.

With My Family

Ask to see some of your baby pictures. Ask family members to share stories of when you were a baby. You are a wonderful creation of God!

I am special.

Faith Words

God the Father
Jesus taught us to call God our loving Father.

God Our Loving Father

Every person is part of God's creation. God created us to be like him. So we are all children of God. God is our loving Father.

Jesus taught us to call God our Father. He taught us to pray this way.

Our Father, in heaven, hallowed be your name.

Based on Luke 11:2

God the Father knows and loves us. We show our love for God our Father by taking care of creation.

How is this family taking care of God's creation?

22

You help all people by taking care of God's world.

Taking Care of God's World

In one puzzle piece draw a picture of something in God's creation that needs care. Then draw how you will take care of it in the other piece.

My Faith Choice

This week I will take care of God's creation. I will try to do what I have drawn in the puzzle.

And now we pray.
God, our God, blesses us.
Psalm 67:7

Chapter Review

Find and circle the faith words in the puzzle.
Use the words in the box to help you.

Creator People Father

X T P E O P L E Y

F A T H E R U M W

W C R E A T O R N

Use the faith words to complete this story.

God is the **C**_____ of
everything that is good.

P_____ are God's creation.

God is our loving **F**_____.

Think and share with your family.
Think of all the wonderful things
God created. Say a prayer of
thanks to God.

Visit our web site at
www.FaithFirst.com

Mary, the Mother of God
A Scripture Story

3

We Pray

Give thanks
to the LORD
who is good,
whose love
is forever!
Based on Psalm 107:1

God sent an
angel to Mary.
The angel had a
special message.
God asked Mary
to be the Mother
of his Son. What
do you know
about this story?

*Mary is the
Mother of God and
our mother too.*

25

Faith Focus

What is the Bible?

Listening to stories about our family can be fun. What is your favorite story about your family? When we share family stories, we learn about each other. When we listen to Bible stories, we learn about God.

A Special Book

The stories in the Bible are about God. The Bible is God's very own word to us. It is a holy book because it is the Word of God.

The stories in the Bible also tell us about people like Abraham, Sarah, Mary, and Joseph. By listening to the stories about these people, we learn about God's love for them and for us.

Learning About God

We learn about God in the Bible. Draw your favorite story from the Bible.

Reading the Word of God

Faith Focus

How did Mary show her love for God?

Faith Words

angel
An angel is a messenger from God.

Mary
Mary is the mother of Jesus, God's Son.

Annunciation
The Annunciation is the announcement of Jesus' birth to Mary by the angel.

When we read the Bible, we learn about God's love for people and their love for him. God sent an **angel** to a young woman named **Mary.** Here is the story.

A Message from God

One day an angel came to Mary. The angel said, "You are blessed, Mary. God has chosen you. You will have a baby. The baby's name will be Jesus. He will be great. He will be the leader of God's own people."

Mary knew that God loved her. Mary spoke to the angel and said, "Yes, I will do what God wants me to do."

Based on Luke 1:26–38

The angel announced to Mary that she would be the mother of Jesus, God's Son. This story is called the **Annunciation.** We honor Mary because she is the Mother of God and our mother too.

Showing Love for God

Mary showed her love for God by saying, "Yes, I will do what God wants me to do." Talk about how the people in the pictures are saying yes to God.

Understanding the Word of God

Mary Trusted God

In this Bible story Mary listened carefully to the angel. This is a sign that Mary trusted God. Mary had **faith** in God.

When we trust someone, we believe that they will keep their promise to us. We believe that they will help us and take care of us.

God asks us to trust him and believe in him. God asks us to have faith in him. We believe in God. We have faith that God will always be with us and help us.

How is the child in this picture showing trust?

What Does This Mean to Me?

Mary showed her faith in God by what she said and did. You show your faith in God by what you say and do too.

Building Faith

Write one thing you can say to show you believe in God. Then draw one thing you can do.

SAY

DO

My Faith Choice

This week I will show I believe in God by

___ saying my prayers each day.

___ being kind to others.

And now we pray.
Trust in the LORD.
Psalm 4:6

Chapter Review

Draw a line to connect the words with their meanings.

Words	Meanings
Mary	A messenger from God
angel	The mother of Jesus, God's Son
Annunciation	The announcement of Jesus' birth to Mary by the angel
faith	Trusting and believing in God

Fill in the blanks.

The  is the

 of G_____.

Think and share with your family.
What can your family tell others about God?

Jesus Is the Son of God

4

We Pray

Blessed be the name of Jesus now and for ever. Amen.

Jesus is the Son of God, who became one of us. What do you know about Jesus?

Mary, Joseph, and Jesus are the Holy Family.

33

Jesus Is with Us

Faith Focus

What do we remember at Christmas?

Faith Words

Son of God
Jesus is the Son of God.

Bethlehem
Bethlehem is the town where Jesus was born.

At Christmas each year we remember the birth of Jesus. It is a wonderful time of the year. God sent Jesus to be with us and show God's love for us. Jesus is the **Son of God.**

Jesus Is Born

The Bible tells us the story of the birth of Jesus.

Mary and Joseph traveled to Bethlehem. There were many people there. They could not find a place to stay. So Mary and Joseph had to stay in a stable. Animals stayed there too.

While they were there, Jesus was born. Mary wrapped her baby in strips of cloth. She laid him in a manger.

Based on Luke 2:1–7

Jesus was born in **Bethlehem.**
Mary, Joseph, and Jesus became
a family.

Telling the Story of Jesus' Birth

Jesus is the Son of God. Number the
sentences in the order they happened.

_____ Jesus was born.

_____ Mary and Joseph traveled
to Bethlehem.

_____ Mary and Joseph stayed
in a stable.

_____ Jesus was laid in a
manger.

_____ Mary and Joseph
could not find a
place to stay.

With My Family

Think of how
you might retell
the story of Jesus'
birth. Tape and
record your story
or make a picture
book of the story.
Share your story
with your family.

Faith Words

Holy Family
   The Holy Family is
   Joseph, Mary, and
   Jesus.

Jerusalem
   Jerusalem is the city
   where Jesus taught
   and helped people.

Temple
   The Temple is the
   place in Jerusalem
   where the Holy
   Family went to
   worship God.

The Trip to the Temple

Jesus was once a child like you. Mary and Joseph took care of him.

Joseph is the foster father of Jesus. Mary is the mother of Jesus. We call Mary, Joseph, and Jesus the **Holy Family.**

At special times the Holy Family traveled with their relatives and friends to **Jerusalem.** They went to the **Temple** to pray to God. Here is a story about one of these times.

Everyone was ready to go home. When Mary and Joseph looked for Jesus, they could not find him.

They finally found him in the Temple. He was listening to the teachers and asking them questions.

When Jesus saw Mary and Joseph, he went with them. They began their trip home together.

Based on Luke 2:43–52

Jesus lived in a family who loved him. The Holy Family loved and took care of Jesus. They helped Jesus to grow up.

Loving Families

Our families help us to grow too. Draw a picture of how your family helps you.

When Jesus grew up, he taught about God. This was the special work God sent him to do.

Everything Jesus said and did tells us about God. Jesus showed us how to love God and others.

Jesus Shows Us How to Live

Jesus showed us how to treat others. He taught us to treat everyone with kindness and **respect.** He helped people who were sick. He fed people who were hungry. Jesus was kind to people others did not like. Jesus prayed for everyone.

We can do what Jesus taught us. We can treat everyone with kindness and respect.

How is the boy in this picture showing kindness and respect?

Jesus came to show God's love for us. You can show love for God and others by your words and actions.

We Love God and Others

In each balloon name ways you show your love for God and others.

My Faith Choice

Choose one of the things you have written in the balloons. Do this to celebrate your love for Jesus this week.

And now we pray.
Teach me, LORD, your way.
Psalm 86:11

Chapter Review

Use the words in the box to complete the puzzle.

Bethlehem	Temple	Holy	Jesus

ACROSS

3. _____ is the town where Jesus was born.

4. _____ is the Son of God.

DOWN

1. We call Mary, Joseph, and Jesus the _____ Family.

2. The place where the Holy Family went to worship God is called the _____.

Fill in the blanks to complete the sentences.

1. The mother of Jesus is

   _____

   _____ .

2. Jesus taught us to treat others with _____

   _____ .

Think and share with your family.

Name ways you and your family can live as Jesus taught us.

ff

Visit our web site at
www.FaithFirst.com

The Good Samaritan
A Scripture Story

5

We Pray

Lord God,
help us to love
you with all our
hearts and to love
others as you
love them.
Amen.

Jesus was a
good storyteller.
Many of the
stories Jesus told
are in the Bible.
Tell about a story
you remember.

*The story of the
Good Samaritan
teaches us how to
care for our
neighbor.*

41

Bible Background

Faith Focus

What do the stories in the Bible tell us?

Faith Words

Old Testament
The Old Testament is the first part of the Bible.

New Testament
The New Testament is the second part of the Bible.

There is something special about our favorite stories. We like to listen to them over and over again.

The Bible

The Bible has many stories. We like to listen to some of those stories over and over again. Bible stories tell us about God and his love for all people.

When we listen to Bible stories, we believe we are listening to God. God is telling us about himself and his love for us. The Bible is the Word of God.

The Parts of the Bible

The Bible has two main parts. The first part is the **Old Testament.** These stories were written before Jesus was born.

The second part is the **New Testament.** This part of the Bible has many stories that Jesus told about God. It also tells us many things Jesus taught about how we are to live as his followers.

With My Family

Ask someone in your family to look at a Bible with you. Find the Old and the New Testaments. Ask them to read one of their favorite Bible stories to you.

Bible

Caring for the Bible

Decorate the cover of this Bible to show that the Bible is special.

Reading the Word of God

Faith Focus
Why did Jesus tell the story of the Good Samaritan?

Faith Words
Samaritan
A Samaritan was someone from the land of Samaria.

The Good Samaritan
Jesus told stories that help us to understand how God wants us to love and care for others. Here is one of those stories.

Robbers attacked a man on a road. They hurt him and took everything he had. They then left him lying on the ground.

A priest came down the road. He walked right by the man and did not help him. A priest's helper then came down the road. He walked right by the man too. He did nothing to help him.

A traveler from the land of Samaria came down the same road. He saw the man lying on the ground. He stopped and wiped the man's wounds and put bandages on them.

He put the man on his donkey and brought him to an inn. "Take care of this man," he said. "I will pay you whatever it costs."

Based on Luke 10:29–37

Jesus was teaching about being a good neighbor. He was teaching how God wants us to treat others.

Being a Good Neighbor

You too can be a good Samaritan. You can help others. Look at each picture. Draw what happens last.

Faith Focus

What does the story of the Good Samaritan teach us about how God wants us to treat others?

Love Your Neighbor

Sometimes it is hard to stop what we are doing and help someone. We might be too busy and not hear them ask us. We might be having too much fun and just do not want to stop.

The Good Samaritan story helps us to know what God wants us to do. God wants us to help one another.

God wants us to take care of one another. God wants us to help other people who need our help. He wants us to help people we like and even people we do not like.

Talk about times you have been helped like the children in the picture.

You can be a good neighbor too. You can show people how much God loves them and cares about them.

Living as a Good Samaritan

Draw one way you can help someone.

My Faith Choice

Think of one way you will help someone this week. Write what you will do on the line.

_____

- - - - - - - - - - - - - - - -

_____

And now we pray.
May all people praise you, God.
Based on Psalm 67:6

Chapter Review

Use the words in the box to fill in the blanks.

New Testament	Old Testament

The Bible tells us about God's love. The first part of the Bible is called the

_____

- -

_____ .

The second part of the Bible is called the

_____

- -

_____ .

Circle yes if the sentence is true. Circle no if the sentence is not true.

1. The Samaritan took care of the hurting man.

    Yes   No

2. Jesus wants us to love one another.

    Yes   No

3. The Samaritan was a bad neighbor.

    Yes   No

Think and share with your family.
Tell about who has been a good neighbor for you and your family.

Visit our web site at
www.FaithFirst.com

Jesus Shows God's Love

6

We Pray

Lord, you are
holy;
you are kind
to us all.
For this we
thank you.
We thank you
above all
for your Son,
Jesus Christ.
Amen.

There are many
Bible stories
about Jesus' love
for people. What
are some ways
Jesus showed his
love for others?

*This cross from
the country of
El Salvador tells us
about Jesus' love.*

Jesus Loves Us

Faith Focus

Why did Jesus die for us?

Faith Words

Crucifixion
  The Crucifixion of Jesus means his being put on a cross to die.

Sometimes someone may give up something to help us. This tells us how much that person really cares about us. What are some things people do to show their love for you?

Jesus Shows His Love

Jesus always shared God's love with people. He was very kind and caring. He helped people who were hurt or sick. He made friends with people others did not like.

Jesus also loved and cared about people who did not like him. He always forgave people who hurt him.

Some people who did not understand Jesus wanted to hurt him. They had Jesus nailed to a cross and he died. This is called the **Crucifixion.**

By dying on the cross, Jesus saved us. Jesus saved us from all the wrong we choose to do. Jesus loved us so much that he gave his life for us.

We Care for Others

Circle the pictures of people showing love and care.

When Jesus died, many people were sad. Then something happened that made them happy.

Jesus Is Alive!

After Jesus died, his friends buried his body in a tomb. Three days later some women who were followers of Jesus went to the place where he was buried. They were surprised at what they saw and heard.

Faith Words

Resurrection
The Resurrection of Jesus is his being raised from the dead.

When the women came to the tomb, they saw men in white robes. "Jesus is not here," the men said. "He has been raised from the dead. Go and tell the other followers of Jesus."

The women told Jesus' other followers what happened. Peter, the leader of Jesus' followers, ran to the tomb. He bent down and looked in. The body of Jesus was not there.

Based on Luke 24:1–12

Jesus was raised from the dead. We call this the **Resurrection** of Jesus.

With My Family

Talk about why Easter is the most joyful time of the year for Christians.

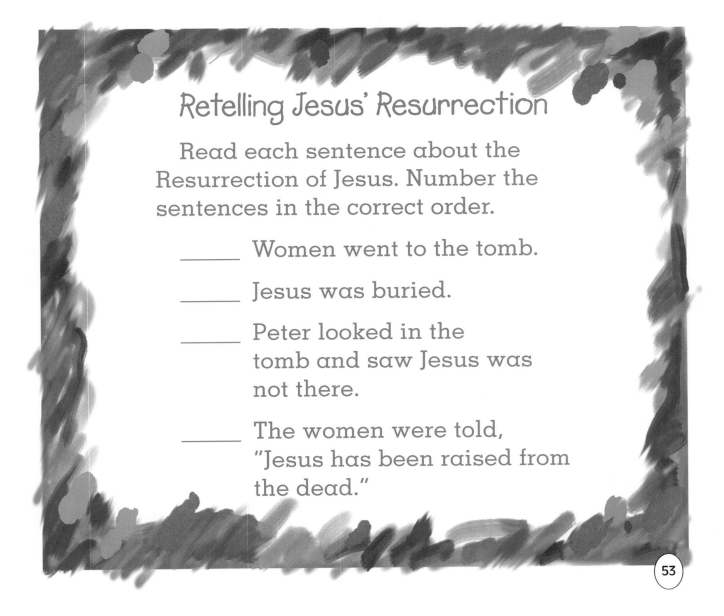

Retelling Jesus' Resurrection

Read each sentence about the Resurrection of Jesus. Number the sentences in the correct order.

_____ Women went to the tomb.

_____ Jesus was buried.

_____ Peter looked in the tomb and saw Jesus was not there.

_____ The women were told, "Jesus has been raised from the dead."

Faith Words

Ascension

The Ascension of Jesus is his return to his Father after he was raised from the dead.

Jesus Returns to His Father

After Jesus was raised from the dead, he stayed with his followers for a while. Jesus told his followers to tell everyone in the world about him. He told them to invite everyone to believe in him and be baptized.

Then one day Jesus returned to his Father in heaven. We call this the **Ascension** of Jesus.

How can you show that you are a follower of Jesus?

You too can tell others about Jesus every day. When you do this, you are doing what Jesus asked all his followers to do.

Telling Others About Jesus

Make a poster that tells others about Jesus. Use your poster as a reminder to act as a follower of Jesus.

My Faith Choice

This week share your poster with someone and tell them about Jesus.

And now we pray.
God's love lasts forever.
Based on Psalm 136:1

Chapter Review

Circle True if the sentence is correct. Circle False if the sentence is not correct.

1. The Resurrection of Jesus is his being raised from the dead.

   True   **False**

2. The Ascension of Jesus is his return to his Father after he was raised from the dead.

   True   **False**

Fill in the circle beside each correct answer.

1. Jesus asked his friends to tell everyone to be his _____.

   ○ Holy Spirit   ○ followers   ○ Father

2. Jesus' _____ is his being put to death on a cross.

   ○ Ascension   ○ Crucifixion   ○ baptism

Think and share with your family.
Name two ways you and your family can be followers of Jesus.

Visit our web site at
www.FaithFirst.com

The Holy Spirit Is Our Helper

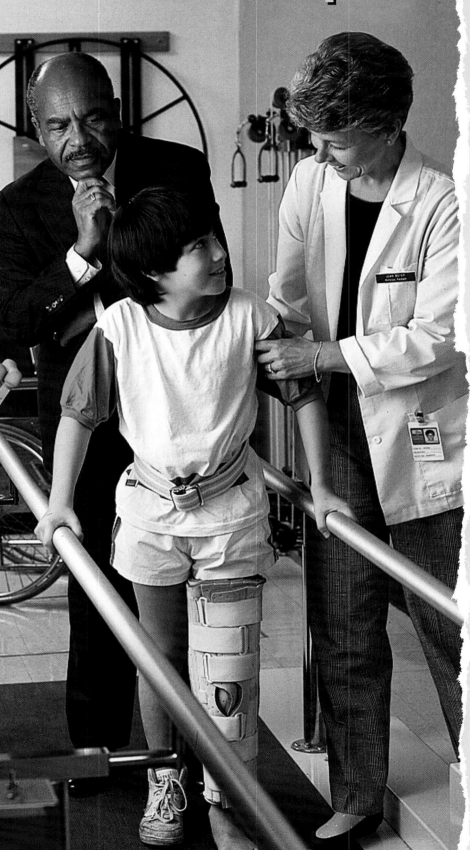

7

We Pray

Blessed be Jesus, who promised to send the Holy Spirit to be with us always so that we can live as God's children. Amen.

Everyone needs helpers. Helpers teach us new things. Who do you think God sent to us to help us?

God helps us through other people.

The Gift of the Holy Spirit

The dove is a symbol for the Holy Spirit.

When we are sad or worried, we are glad someone is at our side to help us. Their words and their smiles help to make us feel better.

Jesus' Promise to Us

When Jesus told his followers that he would be returning to his Father, he saw that they were worried. They did not want Jesus to leave them.

Jesus promised them that God the Father would send them a helper. Jesus told them,

"I will ask the Father to send the Spirit to you. The Spirit will help you. He will be your teacher. He will remind you about everything I told you."

Based on John 14:25–26

Faith Focus

Who did Jesus promise God would send to help the people?

Faith Words

Holy Spirit
The Holy Spirit is the helper Jesus promised would come to help us.

Jesus promised his followers that the **Holy Spirit** would be their teacher. He would help Jesus' followers to understand what Jesus said and did. He would help them to live as Jesus' followers.

The Holy Spirit is our helper too. He is always with us.

Finding the Helper

Color the Xs one color and the Os another color. Find out the name of the helper.

The Holy Spirit is our helper

Faith Words

children of God
Children of God love one another as Jesus taught us to do.

It is fun to receive a gift. Gifts come in all sizes and shapes. Every gift tells us how special we are to the person who gives it to us.

The Holy Spirit Is with Us

God the Father sends us a special gift. It is the gift of the Holy Spirit. The Holy Spirit is a sign of God's love for us.

The Holy Spirit helps us to do what Jesus asked us to do. Jesus told his followers, "Love one another as I love you." When we do what Jesus told us, we are living as **children of God.**

The Holy Spirit Helps Us

3

The Holy Spirit helps us to live as children of God. These pictures show ways the Holy Spirit helps us. Match the sentence that describes each picture.

☐ I help my family.

☐ I help my community.

☐ I say my prayers.

Draw a picture that shows how the Holy Spirit helps you.

Faith Focus

Who is the Holy Trinity?

Faith Words

Holy Trinity
The Holy Trinity is one God in three Persons: God the Father, God the Son, and God the Holy Spirit.

The Holy Trinity

Jesus taught us many things about God. He told us how much God loves us. Jesus taught us there is only one God.

Jesus is the Son of God. Jesus taught us to pray to God the Father. Jesus said he would not leave us alone. God the Holy Spirit would always be with us.

We believe what Jesus told us about God. We believe there is one God in three Persons. We believe in
God the Father,
God the Son, and
God the Holy Spirit.

The **Holy Trinity** is the belief in one God in three Persons.

Who are the three Persons of the Holy Trinity?

God is always with you. The Holy Spirit is your helper.

Praying to the Holy Spirit

Write a prayer asking the Holy Spirit to help you.

Come, Holy Spirit.

Help me to

_____

- -

_____.

Amen.

My Faith Choice

Say the prayer you just wrote each day this week. Try to do what it says.

And now we pray.
Let us give thanks to the Lord our God.

Chapter Review

Write the words to complete the sentences. Use the word box to help you.

1. The helper God sent to his people is the

   Holy _____ .

2. We call the one God in three Persons

   the Holy _____ .

3. The Holy Spirit helps us to live

   as _____ of God.

<table>
<tr><td>children</td></tr>
<tr><td>Trinity</td></tr>
<tr><td>Spirit</td></tr>
</table>

Circle the words that name the three Persons of the Holy Trinity. Write these words on the line.

Q F A T H E R

W S O N E O P

H O L Y C M S

L S P I R I T

_____

_____

Think and share with your family. Talk about some ways the Holy Spirit helps you and your family.

Visit our web site at www.FaithFirst.com

Jesus Gave Us the Church

8

We Pray

God, our loving Father,
we are glad to give you thanks and praise because you love us.
Amen.

We are members of a church family. Who are some of the people you know in your church family?

Each Sunday we gather together to praise and thank God.

65

Faith Focus

What day is the birthday of the Church?

Faith Words

Church

The Church is the People of God.

Pentecost

Pentecost is the day the Holy Spirit came upon the disciples. It is the birthday of the Church.

Birthdays are happy times! It is fun to celebrate birthdays.

The Birthday of the Church

The **Church** is the People of God. The Church has a birthday too. The birthday of the Church is called **Pentecost.** We can read what happened on Pentecost in the Bible.

On the special Jewish holy day of Pentecost, the followers of Jesus were all together. They heard a sound like a strong wind. Small flames settled over each person's head.

The power of the Holy Spirit filled the followers of Jesus. They went out into the streets. Peter, one of Jesus' followers, began telling all the people about Jesus.

Based on Acts of the Apostles 2:1–4, 14

On Pentecost the Holy Spirit came to Jesus' followers. The Holy Spirit helped them and many others to follow Jesus. This is why we call Pentecost the birthday of the Church.

Celebrating the Church

Use the words in the box to finish the birthday poem about the Church.

Pentecost	people	Spirit	Church

The C_____ has a birthday like you and me.

P_____ is its name, you see.

We celebrate that the S_____ came.

And P_____ went out to spread Jesus' name.

Faith Words

Catholic
A Catholic is a Christian who is a member of the Catholic Church.

The Catholic Church

Each family has a name. What is the name of your family? Our church family has a name too.

We belong to the **Catholic** Church. The Catholic family is very big. People all over the world belong to it.

Those who believe in Jesus are part of his family. We believe in Jesus Christ. Together we follow Jesus. We do what Jesus taught us.

We Worship God Together

We share our love for Jesus with one another. We teach others about Jesus. Together we learn about God and his love for us.

We help one another to live as children of God. We pray together. We help others who are poor, sick, hungry, or in need. We share Jesus' love with everyone.

With My Family

List one way each member of your family shares his or her love. Thank one another for what you each do.

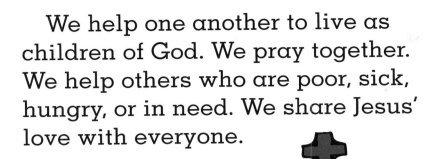

About the Church

Use this code to find a special message.

A	B	C	D	E	F	G	H	I	J	K	L	M
1	2	3	4	5	6	7	8	9	10	11	12	13

N	O	P	Q	R	S	T	U	V	W	X	Y	Z
14	15	16	17	18	19	20	21	22	23	24	25	26

___ ___   ___ ___ ___ ___ ___ ___
23 5   2   5 12 15 14 7

___ ___   ___ ___ ___
20 15   20 8   5

___ ___ ___ ___ ___ ___ ___ ___
3   1 20 8 15 12 9   3

___ ___ ___ ___ ___ ___ .
3   8 21 18 3   8

Faith Words

saints
Saints are holy people the Church honors. They now live with God forever in heaven.

heaven
Heaven is living with God forever.

The Saints Help Us

Some members of the Church are called **saints.** They have died and live with Jesus in **heaven.**

There are many saints named by the Church. Mary, the mother of Jesus, is the greatest saint. Saint Anne was the mother of Mary. Saint Joseph was the husband of Mary. Saint Peter was the first leader of the Church. All the saints show us how to live as children of God.

The Holy Spirit helps the members of the Church on earth. He helps us to live as followers of Jesus. He helps us to be happy with God on earth and in heaven.

This is a statue of Mary as a child with her mother Saint Anne. Who shows you how to live as a child of God?

You are a member of the Church like Mary and the other saints. The saints can help you to live as a follower of Jesus.

Living as a Church Member

In the two large footsteps write ways you can live as a member of the Church.

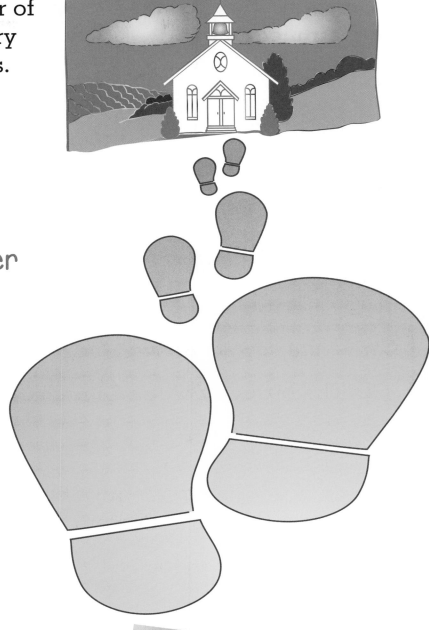

My Faith Choice

Check one thing you will try to do this week.

___ I will help a friend.

___ I will pray to Mary.

___ I will pray to a saint.

And now we pray.
All holy men
and women,
pray for us.
From the Litany of the Saints

71

Chapter Review

Draw a line to connect the words with their meanings.

Pentecost

Catholic

saints

heaven

A Christian who is a member of our Church

The birthday of the Church

Living with God forever

Holy people the Church honors

Circle the correct answer.

1. The birthday of the Church is called _____ .

   Christmas   **Pentecost**

2. On the birthday of the Church, the _____ came to Jesus' followers.

   Holy Trinity   **Holy Spirit**

3. _____ is the greatest saint.

   Peter   **Mary**

Think and share with your family.
Talk about ways the Church is important to you and your family.

Visit our web site at
www.FaithFirst.com

The First Christians Follow Jesus

A Scripture Story

The cross reminds us of Jesus' love for us.

You are a
follower of Jesus.
You pray and
learn with others
in our Church.
What do people
in our Church
do to show they
believe in Jesus?

Faith Focus

What does it mean to be a Christian?

Our families share stories about the things we do. We look at pictures in family photo albums and talk about the people in the pictures.

The First Christians

Faith Words

Christians
Christians believe in and follow Jesus.

Our church family shares stories too. We share stories about what **Christians** did a long time ago. Christians are followers of Jesus. Many stories about what the first Christians did are written down in the New Testament.

The stories in the New Testament help us to understand the lives of the first Christians. What they said and did we still do today. We are Christians too.

Following Jesus

The first Christians followed Jesus. We follow Jesus today. In the road signs write some of the ways we follow Jesus.

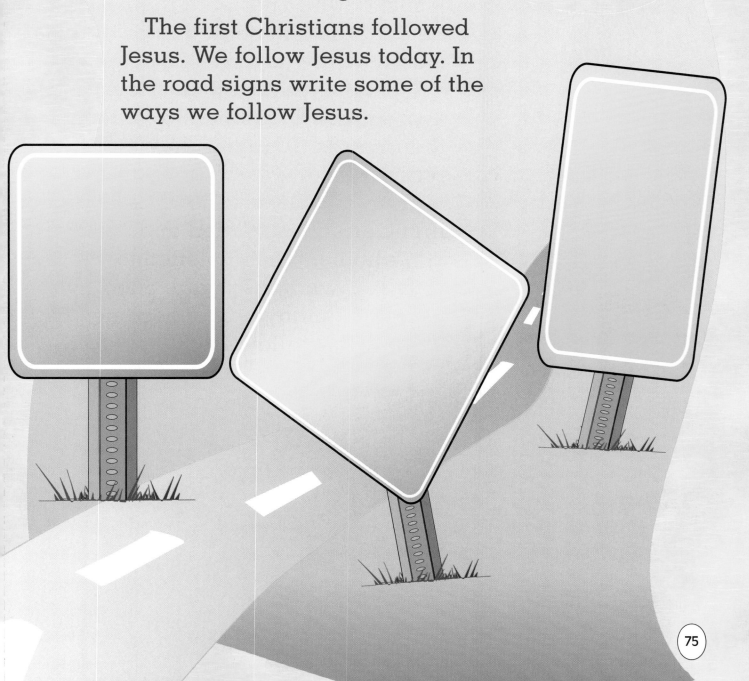

Reading the Word of God

Faith Focus

What did the first Christians do?

The First Christians

This story from the Bible tells us about how the first Christians lived.

Many people came to believe in Jesus. The early Christians spent time learning about what Jesus taught. They sold their belongings and shared their money with one another.

They prayed together. They shared bread together. Joy filled their hearts. Together they praised God.

Many people saw how the first Christians treated one another. They listened to what they said. Soon many others became followers of Jesus.

Based on the Acts of the Apostles 2:42–47

The first Christians showed how much they loved God and one another.

With My Family

Talk about what you do as a family that shows you are a follower of Christ. Think of one more thing you could do this week.

How Christians Live

Read each sentence about the early Christians. Put a ✓ next to each thing that Christians also do today.

Early Christians   **Christians Today**

Prayed together.   ☐

Cared for one another.   ☐

Learned about Jesus.   ☐

Shared what they had with others.   ☐

77

Faith Focus

How did the first Christians show their love for God and one another?

We Love God and Others

Jesus taught us how to live together. He taught us to love God and to love our neighbors.

The first Christians showed their love for God. They prayed each day. They came together to share bread. They thanked God for everything.

The first Christians also showed their love for one another. They shared what they had with others. They helped people in need. Today Christians do the same things.

What do you think the words on the banner mean?

What Does This Mean to Me?

You do some of the same things the first Christians did. You pray. You go to church with your family. You help others.

Living as a Christian

Draw pictures in the photo album that show how you live as a Christian.

My Faith Choice

Check one way you will try to do what the first Christians did.

___ I will pray each day.

___ I will share something with someone.

And now we pray.
Praise the LORD;
the LORD is good!
Psalm 135:3

Chapter Review

Fill in the missing letters to complete the message.

They will know we are

C _ _ _ _ _ _ _ _ _ _ _ _ _ _ _ _ _

by our   l _ _ _ _ _ _ _ .

Read each sentence. Circle yes if it is true. Circle no if it is not true.

1. Christians are followers of Jesus. **Yes   No**

2. The first Christians tried to hurt one another. **Yes   No**

3. Jesus tells us to love God and to love our neighbor. **Yes   No**

Think and share with your family.

Who are the people who have shared God's love with you and your family? Say a prayer of thanks to God for them.

Visit our web site at
www.FaithFirst.com

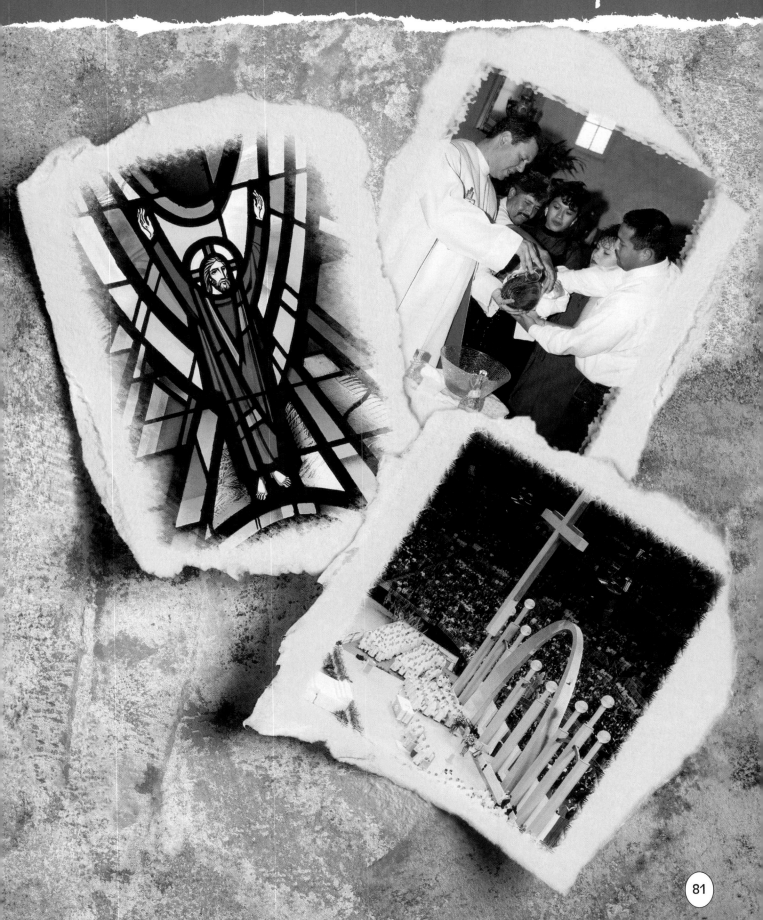

Parent Page—Unit 2: We Worship

Your Role

Young children love to watch for and experience the changes that take place in nature as the seasons change. As the world moves from the warmth and growth of summer to the colder and dormant time of winter, children are keenly aware of the way the world around them is changing in color and texture. Our worship and rituals also have a pattern of change in color and texture as the year progresses. These changes help enrich and deepen our awareness of God's presence in our lives throughout the year. As we move busily from season to season, adults can often lose sight of these changes or take them for granted. Take some time, alone and with your child, to reflect on the seasons of the year and of the church year and think of how they can help deepen your own awareness of God in your life.

What We're Teaching

In this unit the focus is on the patterns and rhythms of the liturgical year. We look at the life of the church community as it gathers to celebrate the liturgy and the sacraments. The students learn about Baptism as a special celebration of God's love. They learn about the Mass as a special time for our church family to come together to worship God. The Scripture lessons deal with Jesus sending the apostles out to teach all people and with Jesus feeding the five thousand. These and all the Scripture lessons in *Faith First* are an opportunity for parents, as well as children, to increase their understanding of the Bible.

Visit our web site at www.FaithFirst.com

What Difference Does It Make?

The lessons in this unit offer wonderful opportunities to talk with your child about your family's experience with the sacraments. Young children enjoy hearing stories and looking at pictures of their own baptism or the baptism of other family members. As your family attends Mass, you might point out the special colors and signs of the church year that you see in your church. The message you send to your child about the importance of the Church's liturgy and sacraments in your daily life is the one that will speak most loudly to your child. If the sacraments are important to you, then your child will also see them as important in his or her life.

Unit Opener Photographs: (top left) stained-glass window of the Risen Christ; (top right) a Baptism; (bottom) Pope John Paul II presides at Mass in Saint Louis, Missouri, 1999.

10

The Church Celebrates All Year

We Pray

**God,
every day I will
bless you.**
Based on Psalm 145:2

There are four seasons of the year. The Church has seasons of the year too. What church seasons do you know about?

We praise and thank God for the beautiful seasons of winter, spring, summer, and fall.

83

The Church's Year

Faith Focus

What are the seasons of the Church's year?

Faith Words

Church's year
The Church's year is made up of five seasons. They are Advent, Christmas, Lent, Easter, and Ordinary Time.

Winter, spring, summer, and fall are the seasons of the year. What do you like best about each season? What colors do you think of when you think of each season?

The Seasons of the Church

The Church has seasons too. The Church's seasons are called Advent, Christmas, Lent, Easter, and Ordinary Time. During each season we celebrate together as God's people.

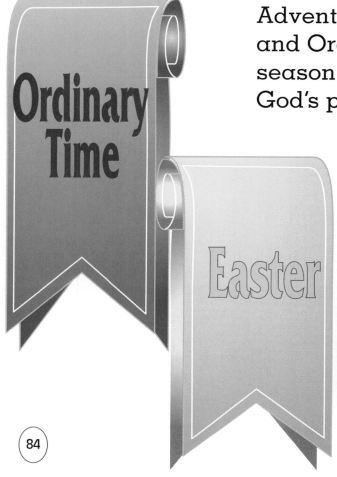

Just as the seasons of the year are filled with special colors, each season of the **Church's year** is filled with special colors too. We can see these colors in our church. White, green, and purple are the colors we use for the seasons of the Church's year. On special days we see gold or red.

Each season of the Church's year tells us something about Jesus. All year long we remember God's love for us.

With My Family

Talk about the sights, sounds, and smells of each of the seasons of the calendar year and of the Church's year.

Celebrating Jesus

Color each letter with one color the Church uses to help us celebrate. The colors are red, white, gold, purple, and green.

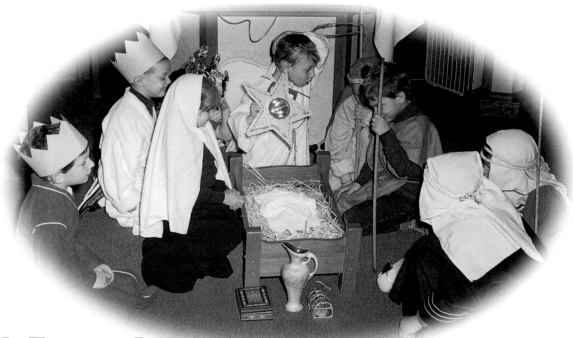

Faith Focus

What do we celebrate during the seasons of Advent and Christmas?

Faith Words

Advent
  Advent is the time of the Church's year when we get ready for Christmas.

Christmas
  Christmas is the time of the Church's year when we remember and celebrate the birth of Jesus.

The Season of Advent

The first season of the Church's year is **Advent.** During Advent we get our hearts ready to remember the birth of Jesus. We use the color purple to celebrate Advent. There are four Sundays in Advent.

The Season of Christmas

Christmas celebrates the birth of Jesus. Jesus is God's greatest gift to us. He is God's Son, who came to live on earth with us.

The Church's celebration of Christmas is not just one day. The season of Christmas lasts about two or three weeks. We use the color white or gold to celebrate Christmas.

Celebrating the Church's Seasons

Write the name of the correct church season on each banner. Color and decorate each banner with the color of the church season.

Faith Focus

What do we celebrate during Lent and Easter?

Faith Words

Lent

Lent is the time of the Church's year when we remember Jesus' life and death.

Easter

Easter is the time of the Church's year when we celebrate that Jesus was raised from the dead.

The Season of Lent

The Church has a special season that helps us to practice being a follower of Jesus. It is called **Lent.** During Lent we try harder to be kind and loving.

Lent also helps us to remember that Jesus died for us. It is a time to get ready for Easter. We ask God to help us to grow closer to Jesus. The color for Lent is purple. This season lasts almost six weeks.

The Season of Easter

During the **Easter** season we celebrate that Jesus was raised from the dead. Jesus gave us the gift of new life. All during Easter we say and sing, "Alleluia!" *Alleluia* means "praise God!" The color for Easter is white.

What reminds you of the Easter season?

When you celebrate the seasons of the Church's year, you celebrate God's love with other people. You remember all that Jesus did for us.

The Church Seasons

In each candle, write or draw ways you celebrate the seasons of the Church's year.

My Faith Choice

Find out what Church season we are celebrating right now. Think of something you can do to show that you know what this season is all about.

And now we pray.
God our Father, all your actions show your love.

Chapter Review

Find and circle the words that tell about the Church's year.

| Advent | Christmas | Lent | Easter |

A D L E N T S W Q
C H R I S T M A S
Y P A D V E N T C
E A S T E R S W L

Use the words in the puzzle to finish these sentences.

A _____ is the season we get ready for Christmas.

C _____ is the season we remember Jesus' birth.

L _____ is the season we get ready for Easter.

E _____ is the season we celebrate Jesus' Resurrection.

Think and share with your family.
What are some special things you can do with your family to celebrate each season in the Church's year?

Visit our web site at
www.FaithFirst.com

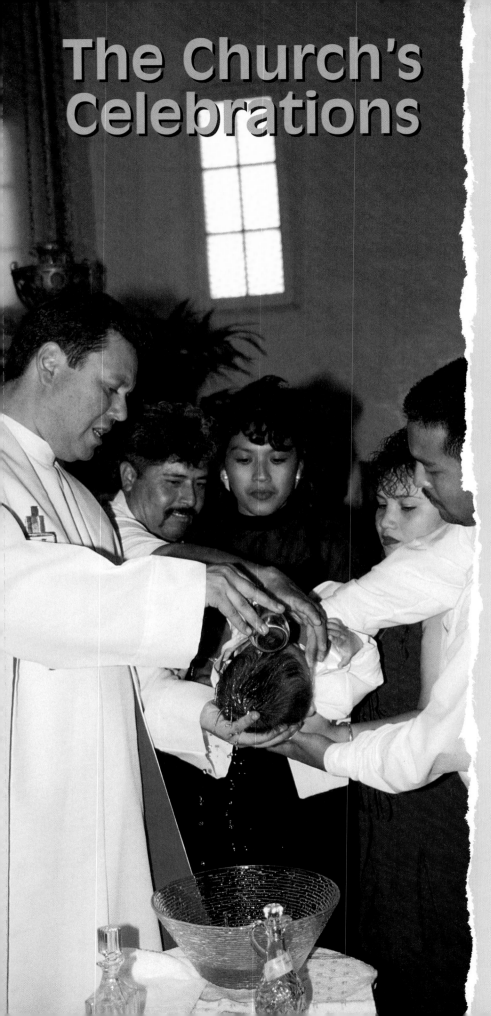

The Church's Celebrations

11

We Pray

How good
to celebrate our
God in song.
Psalm 147:1

Baptism is a
special celebration
of the Church.
What do you
know about
Baptism?

*We are baptized
in the name of the
Father, and of the
Son, and of the
Holy Spirit.*

God Is with Us

Faith Focus

What do the sacraments celebrate?

Faith Words

sacraments

The sacraments are seven special celebrations of the Church. They celebrate that God is with us.

How do you show your love for people? You can spend time together. You can eat together. You can take care of each other. You can forgive each other.

God Shares His Love

God shares his love with us. The Church celebrates this love in the seven **sacraments.**

The sacraments are special celebrations that share God's love and life with us. They help us to remember that God is always with us. Each sacrament helps us to grow closer to God.

Anointing of the Sick

Reconciliation

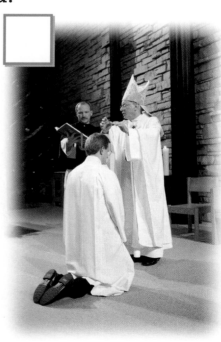

Holy Orders

Celebrating the Sacraments

Circle the sacraments you have received. Put a check mark next to the sacraments you have seen other people receive.

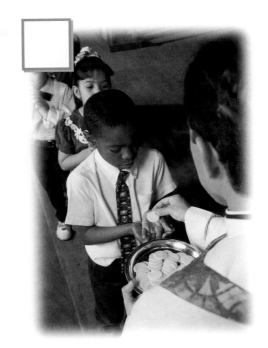

Eucharist

Confirmation

Baptism

Matrimony

We Celebrate Baptism

Baptism is the first sacrament
we celebrate in our church family.
We become members of the
Church at Baptism.

We are baptized with water in
the name of the Holy Trinity. The
priest or deacon says,
I baptize you
in the name of the Father,
and of the Son,
and of the Holy Spirit.
Amen.

Faith Words

Baptism
Baptism is the
sacrament in which
we become
members of the
Church.

All living things need water. The Church uses water to celebrate Baptism. This shows we are receiving new life with God. At Baptism we receive the gift of the Holy Spirit. We celebrate that we are children of God.

We also wear white clothing. This tells everyone that God shares his life and love with us when we are baptized.

With My Family

Make a prayer card for your godparents or family members. Thank them for their help and care for you.

Celebrating Baptism

At Baptism we become members of the Church. Write a word or group of words about Baptism in each drop of water.

95

Faith Focus

What happens when we become members of our church family?

Jesus Is the Light

At Baptism we are born into our church family. After we are baptized with water, the priest or deacon anoints, or rubs, our head with a special oil. This shows that we are members of the Church. We belong to Christ. We are followers of Jesus. We are to live as Jesus taught us.

We also receive a lighted candle. The candle was lit from the Easter candle. We bring the light of Jesus to everyone.

Jesus is the Light of the world. What can you say or do to be a light in the world?

At Baptism you became a follower of Jesus. Read the rebus about your Baptism with someone in your family.

My Baptism

My name is _____ .

I was baptized with  .

I received a lighted baptismal , the light of Jesus.

I wore a baptismal , a sign of my new life in Christ.

I am God's  .

My Faith Choice

I will live as a follower of Jesus this week by

_____ doing an extra chore to help my family.

_____ praying for a friend.

And now we pray. May I walk always as a child of the light.

Chapter Review

Draw a line to connect the words with their meanings.

Words	Meanings
sacraments	This is the first sacrament of the Church.
Baptism	There are seven of these celebrations.
water	This is used at Baptism to show that we are receiving new life from God.

Circle the correct answer.

1. At Baptism we receive the _____ .

    Holy Spirit   **Church**

2. The lighted _____ reminds us that we bring the light of Jesus to everyone.

    candle   **oil**

Think and share with your family.
Share stories about the baptisms of different family members.

Come, Follow Jesus

A Scripture Story

12

We Pray

We believe in you, Lord Jesus Christ. Amen.

The Bible tells many stories about people becoming Jesus' followers. Name a person in the Bible that was a follower of Jesus.

Jesus died and was raised from the dead.

Tell the Good News

Faith Focus

What does Jesus call people to do?

We all like to hear good news. We like to share good news with others too. What is some good news you would like to share today?

The Good News of Jesus

The followers of Jesus shared the good news about Jesus. One of Jesus' followers was named Matthew. He told about Jesus in the **Gospel** according to Matthew. The word *gospel* means "good news."

Faith Words

Gospel
   The word *gospel* means "good news."

Matthew shares many stories about Jesus with us. Some of these stories tell about Jesus helping people. Other stories tell about Jesus teaching people.

The main story Matthew tells is about Jesus dying and being raised from the dead. This is the good news that Matthew wants to share with everyone.

With My Family

Write the words *Good News* on a piece of paper. Write or draw some good news about Jesus. Share it with your family.

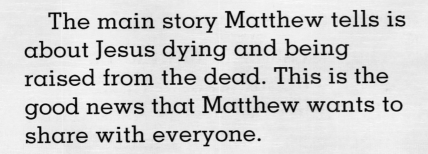

Telling the Good News

We can tell the good news about Jesus today. Make a poster to tell about Jesus. Share the Good News!

Reading the Word of God

Tell the Good News

The last story in Matthew's Gospel is about Jesus returning to his Father. Before his Ascension, Jesus gave his followers, or **disciples,** an important message.

The disciples went to a mountain. Jesus came to them and told them to tell everyone about him. Jesus said,

"Go to every land you can. When you get there, invite all people to become my followers. Baptize them in the name of the Father, and of the Son, and of the Holy Spirit. Teach them what I have taught you."

Based on Matthew 28:16–20

Jesus asked his disciples to baptize people. Through Baptism people become followers of Jesus.

| God |
| baptize |
| Jesus |
| loves |

Sharing Good News About Jesus

Jesus asked his disciples to tell everyone about him. Fill in what the disciples might have said about Jesus.

"Jesus is the Son of _____ ."

"Follow _____ ."

"I _____ you in the name of the Father, and of the Son, and of the Holy Spirit. Amen."

"Jesus said, 'God _____ us.'"

Faith Focus

Who are Christians?

Faith Words

Christians
   Christians are
   followers of
   Jesus Christ.

Followers of Christ

After Jesus returned to his Father in heaven, the disciples did what he asked them to do. They preached in small villages and large cities. People who believed in Jesus were baptized.

Those who were baptized became known as **Christians.** They were called Christians because they were the followers of Jesus Christ.

How does a Christian act?

You can do what Jesus asked the disciples to do. You can tell other people the good news about Jesus.

Tell the Good News

You are a disciple. Write what you would tell other people about Jesus.

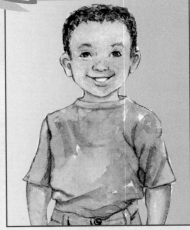

Who is Jesus?

My Faith Choice

Share what you have written about Jesus with someone this week. Write that person's name on the line.

_____

- - - - - - - - - - - - - - -

And now we pray. My mouth will speak your praises, LORD.

Psalm 145:21

105

Chapter Review

Solve the
crossword puzzle.

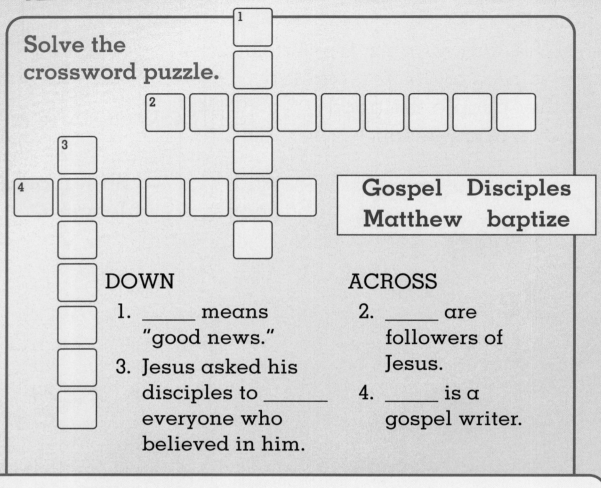

Gospel   Disciples
Matthew   baptize

DOWN

1. _____ means
   "good news."
3. Jesus asked his
   disciples to _____
   everyone who
   believed in him.

ACROSS

2. _____ are
   followers of
   Jesus.
4. _____ is a
   gospel writer.

Circle the correct answer.

1. The return of Jesus to his Father is called his
   _____ .

   Baptism   **Ascension**

2. The followers of Jesus are called _____ .

   Christians   **preachers**

Think and share with your family.
Name ways you and your
family tell others about Jesus.

We Celebrate at Mass

13

We Pray

God,
our loving Father,
we are glad
to give you
thanks and
praise because
you love us.
Amen.

Our church
family comes
together at Mass.
What are some
of the things you
see and hear
at Mass?

*People gather with
Pope John Paul II
to celebrate Mass in
Saint Louis, Missouri,
January, 1999.*

We Gather for Mass

Faith Focus
What is the Mass?

Faith Words
Mass
We gather at Mass to praise and thank God.

Thank you! Thank you! In many ways we can thank people for their kind words and actions.

We Gather as God's People

One way our church family gives thanks to God is by celebrating the **Mass** together. At Mass we gather to praise and thank God our Father. We worship God.

We gather as the People of God. We begin by blessing ourselves, "In the name of the Father, and of the Son, and of the Holy Spirit. Amen."

Sometimes the priest will sprinkle holy water over all the people at the beginning of Mass. This reminds us of our Baptism. It helps us to remember that we belong to Jesus and are members of the Church.

Worshiping God

We gather at Mass to worship God. Circle every other letter. Copy the letters on the lines to find a message about the Mass. The first letter is circled for you.

T (A) B T R M G A D S N S
X W L E R G O I Q V Y E
Z T D H R A F N Q K N S
B T D O Z G R O Z D P

_____

- -

_____

- -

_____

We Listen to God's Word

At Mass we also listen to stories from the Bible. The Bible is the Word of God.

Each Sunday at Mass we listen to three readings. The readings tell us about God's love for us. The third reading is always a story about Jesus. It is from the Gospel.

Then the priest or deacon helps us to understand the readings. He helps us to understand what God is saying to us.

We come to know and love God even more. We learn how to live as Jesus taught us. We try to decide ways we will show God how much we love him.

Living the Gospel

The Gospel tells us what Jesus said and did. We try to live as Jesus taught us. After each sentence write or draw what you can do.

With My Family

Share the good news by talking to your family about a Bible reading you heard at Mass. You can draw a picture, tape the story, or make a storybook.

Jesus taught us to tell others about him.

Jesus taught us to love one another.

Faith Words

Last Supper
The Last Supper is the last meal Jesus ate with his disciples before he died.

Eucharist
The Eucharist is the sacrament in which we receive the Body and Blood of Christ.

A Special Meal

At Mass we do what Jesus taught us. On the night before he died, Jesus ate a special meal with his disciples. We call that meal the **Last Supper.**

At the Last Supper Jesus took bread and said,
"This is my body."
Then he took the cup of wine and said,
"This is my blood."

Based on Matthew 26:26–29

At Mass we remember and do what Jesus did at the Last Supper. We celebrate **Eucharist.** The bread and wine become the Body and Blood of Christ. Jesus is present with us.

What do we remember and do at Mass?

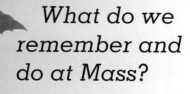

When you are at Mass, you listen to God's Word and celebrate the Eucharist. You praise and thank God.

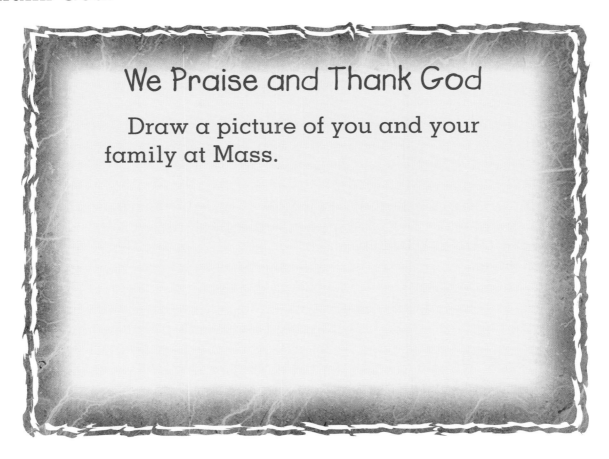

We Praise and Thank God

Draw a picture of you and your family at Mass.

My Faith Choice

Check one way you will show your love for God this week.

_____ I will listen to the readings at Mass.

_____ I will say a special thank-you prayer to God.

And now we pray.
We thank you, God our Father, for your Son, Jesus Christ.

Chapter Review

Draw a line to match the words with their meanings.

Words	Meanings
Last Supper	Gathering to praise God
Mass	Body and Blood of Christ
Eucharist	The meal Jesus ate before he died

Complete each sentence.

1. We gather at Mass to
   _____

   _____ .

2. We listen to stories from the Bible at
   _____

   _____ .

3. At Mass the bread and wine become the Body
   _____
   ----
   and Blood of _____ .

Think and share with your family.
How can you and your family make Mass more meaningful for the whole family?

Visit our web site at
www.FaithFirst.com

Jesus Feeds a Crowd

A Scripture Story

14

We Pray

God's love
lasts
forever.
Based on Psalm 136:25

The Bible has many stories about how Jesus took care of people. What are some ways that Jesus helped people?

One day Jesus fed many people with five loaves of bread and two fish.

Bible Background

Faith Focus

Why did Jesus share food with others?

Faith Words

Sea of Galilee
The Sea of Galilee is the area where Jesus taught and helped people.

The smell of fresh warm bread can make us feel hungry. The sound of crunchy red apples may bring a smile to our faces. Food is good for us and helps us to grow.

The Food of Jesus' Time

Some of the food we eat today is like the food Jesus ate. Jesus and the people at that time ate many foods like bread, fruit, and fish.

Fish was an important food because the people lived near water. Many people were fishermen. They would fish in the **Sea of Galilee** for their food.

Jesus shared food with his followers. Jesus fed people to share God's love.

Sharing God's Love

In one boat write or draw one way Jesus helped people. In each of the other boats, write or draw one way you can help people.

With My Family

Collect some food in a bag or basket. With your family take it to your church or a food pantry to share with people who are hungry.

117

Faith Focus

How did Jesus care for others?

Jesus Feeds the People

Jesus and his twelve special followers went to a town. It was near the Sea of Galilee. About five thousand people followed them there.

That evening, his followers said, "Send the people away. They must go and buy food."

Jesus said, "Give them something to eat."

"We have only five loaves of bread and two fish," the followers said.

Jesus blessed the bread and the fish. His followers gave the food to the people.

Everyone ate until they were full. Then Jesus' followers filled twelve baskets with leftovers.

Based on Luke 9:10–17

The followers of Jesus shared bread and fish. All the people ate and were filled.

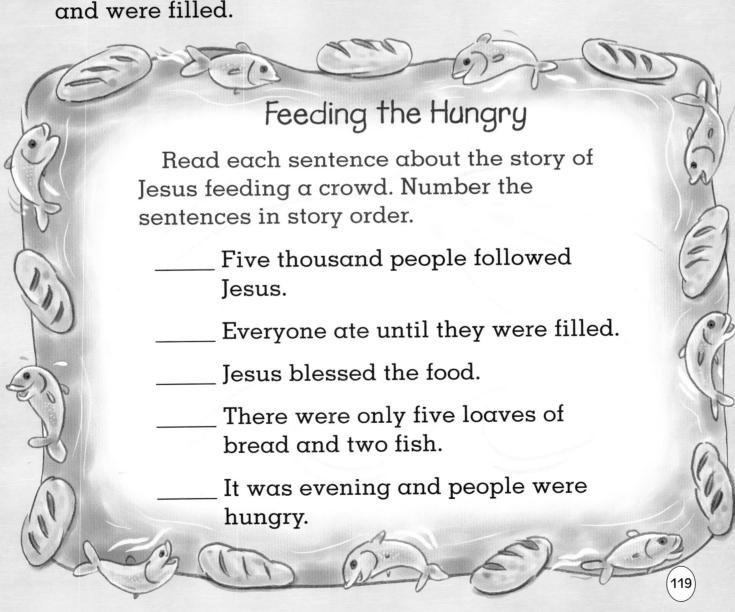

Feeding the Hungry

Read each sentence about the story of Jesus feeding a crowd. Number the sentences in story order.

_____ Five thousand people followed Jesus.

_____ Everyone ate until they were filled.

_____ Jesus blessed the food.

_____ There were only five loaves of bread and two fish.

_____ It was evening and people were hungry.

Understanding the Word of God

Faith Focus

What did Jesus teach us about God?

Jesus Shares God's Love

God cares for everyone. This story shows how Jesus shared God's love with the people.

Many people had been listening to Jesus. They were hungry and had no food. Jesus turned the bread and fish into enough food to feed a big crowd of people. Everyone ate until they were filled.

Jesus took care of the people. Jesus asks us to take care of one another too. This is one way we can share God's love with others.

How is the girl in the picture sharing God's love?

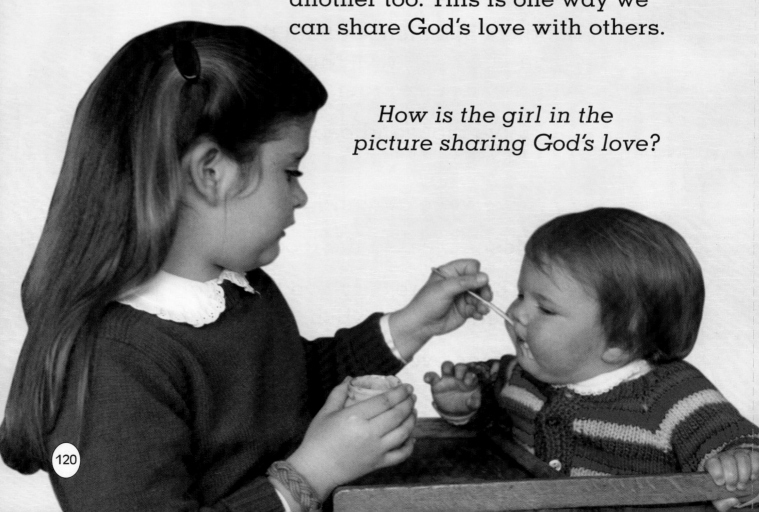

120

Jesus saw that the people were hungry. Jesus fed the people to show that God cares for them. Like Jesus, you can show God's love and care for others.

Caring for Others

Check what you can do to care for someone else.

_____ I can help out at home.

_____ I can play fairly.

_____ I can be extra nice to someone.

_____ I can say a prayer.

My Faith Choice

Look at the things you have checked in the fish. Try to do what you checked this week.

And now we pray.
Blessed be the LORD.

Psalm 28:6

121

Chapter Review

Find the words in the puzzle about Jesus caring for others.

```
B J E S U S T R A B K
C H U R C H R Y T B A
Z R B F I S H L T O P
W V A P B B R E A D L
B L E S S E D C N P R
```

Church

Jesus

Fish

Blessed

Bread

Number the sentences in the correct order.

_____ Jesus and many of his followers lived near the Sea of Galilee.

_____ They became very hungry.

_____ One day many people followed Jesus.

_____ Jesus blessed the bread and fish.

_____ He gave the food to his followers to share with the people.

Think and share with your family.
Name ways you and your family can show God's loving care for one another.

Visit our web site at
www.FaithFirst.com

Parent Page—Unit 3: We Live

Your Role

How does your child learn right from wrong? You teach it to him or her. It sounds simple, but that is how it works. As your children grow they learn what is right and wrong from your voice, from "time outs," from conversations with you, and so forth. Gradually they learn to discern the difference between doing something accidentally and doing something on purpose. From there children learn to think before they act, to see alternatives and options, and to see the consequences of their actions. This moral growth happens gradually and there is no one more important in this formational process than you. Your child watches what you do—how you act, how you make decisions—and learns from that.

As your child is learning about morality in this unit, it is an ideal time for you to talk together about the many decisions that your child or you make each day. Reflect on what was decided, what could have been decided, and why. Your child will learn from you how to decide between one thing and another or from among a multitude of choices. That is a good lesson for life.

What We're Teaching

The focus of this unit is morality. The children learn that each person is a special gift of God created out of God's great love for each of us. They will learn that God asks us to take good care of ourselves and all other people and to share our love with everyone. They learn that our family and our church community help us learn how to live as children of God and support us as we try to do what is right. The Scripture stories center on Moses in the Old Testament and on Jesus' blessing of the children in the New Testament.

Visit our web site at www.FaithFirst.com

What Difference Does It Make?

At the very heart of making good moral choices is an understanding of the sacredness of all life. When people see themselves and others as unique and precious gifts, they will be more likely to make moral decisions that protect and preserve the dignity and worth of each human person. As a parent you can help your child see and understand each person's uniqueness and specialness in God's eyes. You do this every day by how you interact with others in your daily life—at the store, at home, and even as you drive your car. Your child is watching and learning from you all the time, and often your actions speak louder than your words. Take some time to reflect on how your interactions with others help your child grow in an awareness of himself or herself and others as precious children of God.

Unit Opener Photographs: (top left) stained-glass window of Jesus and the children; (top right) child caring for baby brother; (bottom) family spending time together.

We Live as Children of God

15

We Pray

Loving God,
you created all
the people of
the world,
and you know
each of us
by name.
Bless us with
your love.

We are God's children. What do you think it means to be a child of God?

God gives us the gift of life.

God Made Us

There are many kinds of people. People speak different languages and have different color skin. But we are all created and loved by God.

Children of God

God created people out of love. God is love. Because of God's love, he created us in his image and likeness. In the Bible we read,

God created people in his image.

Based on Genesis 1:27

We are children of God. We are part of a family. We are all part of God's family.

Children of God love God and each other. They know that all people are created in God's image.

Living as Children of God

We are all part of God's family. Draw a picture that shows you as a member of God's family.

With My Family

Make a poster with the words *Children of God.* Draw people living as children of God. Make sure you draw yourself, because you are a child of God too.

127

Our Gift of Life

God is our loving Father. God gives each of us the gift of life. We are his children. Children of God love God, other people, and themselves.

God asks us to take care of the gift of life he gives us. God wants us to take care of ourselves. When we take care of ourselves, we love ourselves as God wants us to.

Children of God also love other people. We show our love for others in many ways. Kind words and actions let others know we care about them.

Children of God take very good care of the gift of life that God shares with us. By doing this we are showing our love for God, for ourselves, and for others.

Taking Care of God's Gifts

In the first package draw or write how you can care for yourself. In the second package draw or write how you can care for someone else.

We Show Our Love for God

God created us because he loves us. God knows each of us by name. God made us to know and love him too.

Faith Focus

Why did God make us?

Jesus taught us about God's love and showed us how to love God. When we pray, we are showing our love for God. When we help to do God's work on earth, we are showing our love for God. Another way of saying this is that we are serving God and others.

God loves us so much he wants us to be happy with him always. God created us to be happy with him forever in heaven.

How are the people in the pictures showing their love for God?

130

What Does This Mean to Me?

God made you and loves you. You are a child of God.

Praying for Others

God's children live all over the world. Write a prayer for God's children.

Dear God,

____

I ______________________________.

____

Help ______________________________.

____

Thank you for ______________________________.

Amen.

My Faith Choice

This week I will live as a child of God by

____

______________________________.

And now we pray.

May God bless us.

Psalm 67:8

Use this code to find an important message about ourselves.

A	B	C	D	E	F	G	H	I	J	K	L	M
1	2	3	4	5	6	7	8	9	10	11	12	13

N	O	P	Q	R	S	T	U	V	W	X	Y	Z
14	15	16	17	18	19	20	21	22	23	24	25	26

___ ___   ___ ___ ___   ___ ___ ___
23 5   1 18 5   1 12 12

,

___ ___ ___ ___   ___ ___ ___ ___ ___ ___ ___ ___ .
7 15 4 19   3   8   9 12 4 18 5 14

Finish each sentence.

1. Heaven is

_____

_____ .

2. God loves us because

_____

_____ .

Think and share with your family.

How do you and your family show others you are children of God?

Visit our web site at
www.FaithFirst.com

We Live as a Family

16

We Pray

May God join us together. Amen.

We belong to a family. Our families teach us about God and God's family. What does your family teach you about God?

Families celebrate God's love.

133

Family Love

Faith Focus

How do families show their love?

With My Family

Ask to see photographs of the wedding of someone in your family. Ask them to tell you about that special day. Say a prayer to God thanking him for your family.

We all want friends. Friends make us happy. When we meet a very special person, we may become best friends. Isn't it fun to be friends?

Families Show Their Love

When a grown man and woman become best friends, sometimes they want to be together always. They begin to plan their life together. Their parents, the priest, and the Church help them. They love each other and they love God. God will bless them and their love in the sacrament of Matrimony.

Married love is shared by a husband and a wife. They share their love with God.

God gives a husband and a wife a wonderful gift, the gift of children. Together with their children they become a family.

Members of a family care for one another. The family is a blessing from God!

Sharing Family Love

Read this poem about family love.
Fill in the blanks with rhyming words.

Families, families everywhere
show each other love and

_____

- -

_____ .

They tell us of God's love, you see.
God loves each of us, you and

_____

- -

_____ .

Faith Focus

What do our families teach us?

Families Help One Another

Families are signs of God's love. Families teach us about God's love. They share love with God and with one another. Each person in the family is important. Each person is a child of God.

Families often help one another. They take care of each other. They respect one another.

Parents help their children and keep them safe. People in families say kind words to one another.

Families pray together. They ask God to help them to be loving and kind. Loving families love God and each other.

Living Family Love

Write how the families in each picture are sharing God's love.

_____

_____

_____

_____

_____

_____

_____

Faith Focus

How do our families help us to live our faith?

God's Family

Our families also teach us about God's family. Our families teach us about the Holy Family. Mary, Joseph, and Jesus are the Holy Family.

Our families teach us about other people who loved God too. They teach us about saints. Saints follow Jesus. They share God's love with others.

Our families help us to live our faith. With our church family we learn to care for others. We give food to the poor. We visit sick friends. We pray for all God's people.

The Holy Family showed their love for God in many ways. How does your family show its love for God?

You are part of a family. You share God's love with your family members.

Sharing Family Love

Learn this sign language.
Teach it to your family members.

I **love** **you.**

God **loves** **you.**

My Faith Choice

Think of one way you will share God's love with a family member. Make a card telling that person what you will do.

And now we pray.
Show your wonderful love.
Psalm 17:7

Chapter Review

Complete the sentences, using the words in the box.

sacrament	blessing	families

1. God blesses the love of a man and woman

   _____

   in the _____ of Matrimony.

   _____

2. Our _____
   teach us about God's love for us.

   _____

3. Families are a _____
   from God.

Unscramble the letters to find the messages.

_____ help us to live our _____ .
Fmilseia   **thaif**

Each person in a family is a _____ of God.
                                ldchi

Think and share with your family.

Talk about some of the people in your church family that help you to know God. Make a prayer card for them.

Visit our web site at
www.FaithFirst.com

We Live as a Community

We Pray

O Lord,
how great is
your kindness
which you have
shown to us.

As children of
God we belong
to a family. We
also belong to a
church community.
How does our
community
help us?

*We gather with our
church community
to celebrate our love
for God.*

Faith Focus

Who is God's family?

People may be different colors. They may speak in different ways too.

We Are All Special

God makes each of us different. But he also makes us alike in many ways. God gives each of us special gifts. Some people sing. Some people bake. Some people dance. God loves each of us. We are his creation.

With My Family

Name the special gifts that God gave you and your family members. List each person's name and their gift on a piece of construction paper. Hang it where everyone will see it to remind them of God's gifts.

God wants us to live as a family, God's family. He sent his Son, Jesus, to show us how to live as children of God. Jesus gave us the gift of the Church. The Church helps us to live as God's family.

Sharing Our Gifts

God made each person special. Look at the people in the pictures. Talk about what gift each child is using. In the box draw a gift that you can share.

Laws Help Us

Families have rules. Rules are good. Rules help the family to work together. Rules keep us safe.

Your community has special rules called laws. A **law** is a rule that is good for everyone.

God has laws for us too. God's laws help us to live together. These laws tell us to love and care for everyone.

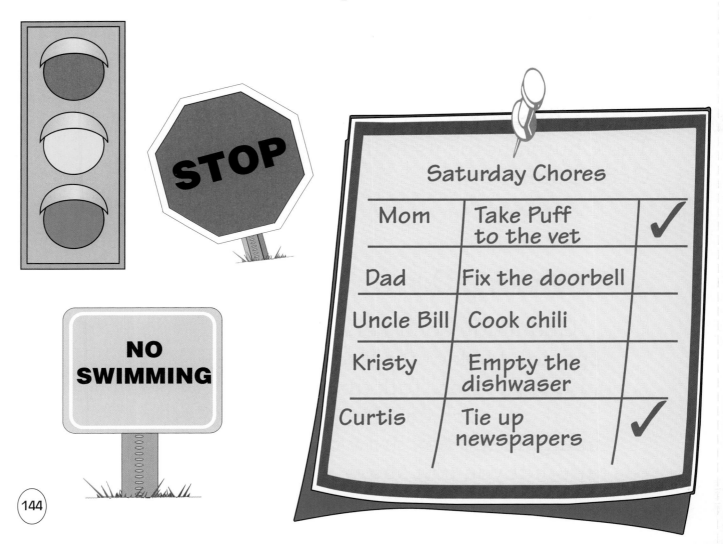

STOP

NO SWIMMING

Saturday Chores		
Mom	Take Puff to the vet	✓
Dad	Fix the doorbell	
Uncle Bill	Cook chili	
Kristy	Empty the dishwaser	
Curtis	Tie up newspapers	✓

God's laws help us to know right and wrong. They help us to make good choices. God's laws help us to choose to follow Jesus.

Sharing God's Love

Follow the road map of your community. At each place, stop and write a way you can live God's laws.

1 _____

_____

2 _____

_____

3 _____

_____

Faith Words

vocation
A vocation is God's call to live your life in a certain way.

We Follow God's Call

God asks us to live in a certain way. God wants all people to love him with their whole heart. He wants all people to love others as they love themselves.

When we love God, we live our lives with love. When we live our lives with love, we are kind to others. We take good care of ourselves. We are living our **vocation.** Love is our life's work.

How are the people in the pictures answering God's call?

You are part of a community. By following God's laws, you can live a life of love.

Living God's Laws

God wants us to love and care for everyone. Finish each sentence to tell what you can do to share God's love.

1. I can share my _____ .

2. I can help by _____ .

3. I can pray for _____ .

My Faith Choice

Look at the chart above. Put a check (✔) next to what you will do to show God's love this week.

And now we pray.
"Keep the way of the Lord."

Use the clues to solve the puzzle.

DOWN

1. This is living a life of love.
3. This is the place we come to worship God.

ACROSS

2. These are God's rules that help guide us.
4. You are part of this special kind of group.

laws   community

church   vocation

Circle the correct answer.

1. God wants us to live a life of _____ .

    unhappiness   love

2. God gives us _____ to help us to live.

    laws   toys

Think and share with your family.

What are some of your family rules that are also God's laws?

Visit our web site at
www.FaithFirst.com

Moses Leads God's People

A Scripture Story

18

We Pray

God said to Moses, "I will be with you."

Based on Exodus 3:12

God gives us special people to help us. Who are some special people who take care of you?

Moses led God's people through the desert.

Faith Focus

Who is Moses?

There are many people in our community who take care of us. God gives us people to take care of us. Parents, grandparents, doctors, teachers, priests, and sisters all help us.

A Special Leader

God chooses special people to take care of his family. A long, long time ago, God chose Moses to be a leader of God's people.

Moses was afraid he would not be a good leader. But God told Moses he would always be with him.

Moses trusted God. He listened to God and took care of the people.

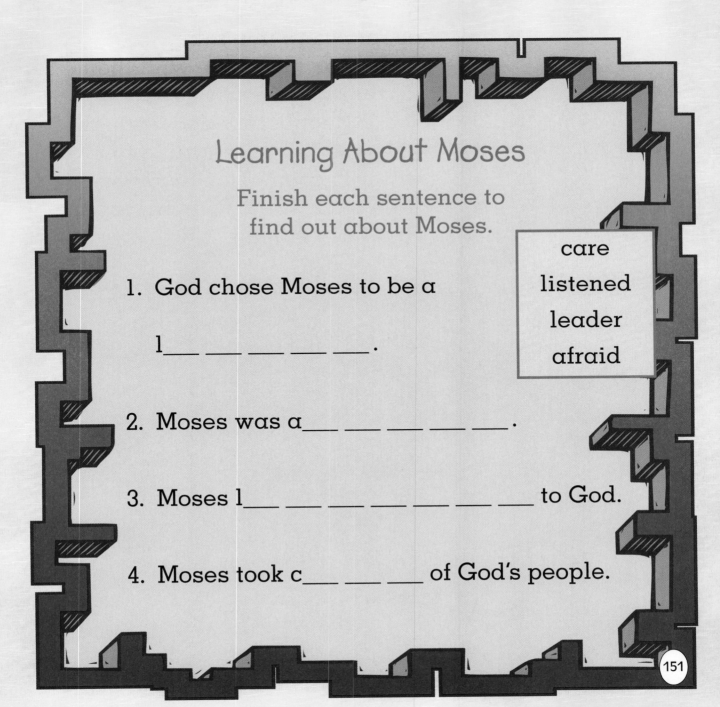

Learning About Moses

Finish each sentence to find out about Moses.

care

listened

leader

afraid

1. God chose Moses to be a

   l__ __ __ __ __ .

2. Moses was a__ __ __ __ __ .

3. Moses l__ __ __ __ __ __ __ to God.

4. Moses took c__ __ __ of God's people.

Reading the Word of God

Faith Focus

How did God take care of his people?

Moses Leads God's People

In the Old Testament of the Bible, we read about Moses. God told Moses to take his people to a new land.

A great crowd of people gathered to make the trip. The people were in a hurry to leave. They took very little with them for their journey.

The people traveled through the desert. It was hard to find water to drink. They had very little food. They were hungry. God heard them!

God said to Moses,
"I will send bread from
heaven for you." God did! The
next morning, the ground was
covered with bread. Everyone
had enough to eat!

Based on Exodus 16:4

God fed Moses and the people.
God took good care of his people.

Leading the People of God

Moses was the leader of God's
people. Help Moses lead the people
through the desert.

God Cares for His People

God showed Moses and his people the way to a new land. God gave them food when they were hungry. He watched over them and kept them safe. They were his people, and he took good care of them.

God loves his people. The story of Moses in the Bible shows us God's great love. It shows that God always takes care of his people.

We are God's people! God cares for us because he loves us. Everywhere we can see signs of God's love.

How does God show his love for you?

You can help to take care of God's people as Moses did.

Taking Care of Others

God takes care of you. Write ways you can care for others in these love coupons.

With My Family

Draw pictures of ways that God has taken care of you and your family. Say a prayer to tell God how much you love him.

Love Coupon

Name of person

_____

I will care for you by

_____

Your name

_____

Love Coupon

Name of person

_____

I will care for you by

_____

Your name

_____

My Faith Choice
Circle the coupon you can do this week.

And now we pray.
"The Lord is with you."

Luke 1:28

Draw a line to match the persons with the Who Am I? clues.

Persons	Who Am I?
Moses	I chose Moses to lead my people to a new land.
God	We followed Moses because we trusted God.
God's people	I led the people through the desert.

Solve the puzzle to find out the message of the story of Moses.

A	B	C	D	E	F	G	H	I	J	K	L	M
1	2	3	4	5	6	7	8	9	10	11	12	13

N	O	P	Q	R	S	T	U	V	W	X	Y	Z
14	15	16	17	18	19	20	21	22	23	24	25	26

__ __ __   __ __ __ __ __
7 15 4   20 1 11 5 19

__ __ __ __   __ __   __ __ .
3 1 18 5   15 6   21 19

Think and share with your family.

Name ways you and your family are leaders in your church.

We Love God

19

We Pray

Lord God, heavenly King, Almighty God and Father, we worship you, we give you thanks, we praise you! Amen.

We follow rules to be safe and to care for others. God gave us rules to help us to love one another. What are some of God's rules?

People in our community help to keep us safe.

God's Commandments Help Us

Faith Focus

Why did God give us commandments?

Faith Words

Ten Commandments
The laws God
gave to Moses
are called the Ten
Commandments.

Red means stop. Yellow means careful, and green means go. We follow the traffic rules to help keep us safe. Rules at home, at school, and in our community help us to care for ourselves and others.

The Ten Commandments

God gave us rules to help us to show love and kindness too. God's rules are called commandments. In the Bible we learn that God gave us the **Ten Commandments.**

The Ten Commandments help all people to live as God's family. These rules show us the way to love God and others.

With My Family

Talk about how people are alike and how they are different. Remember that God loves each of us in a special way.

Living as God's Family

Write one of the rules that help you show love and kindness.

_____

- -

_____

Draw one way you can live that rule.

We Love God

The Ten Commandments help us to show our love for God. We love God more than anything or anyone else. God loves us very much too.

We show our love for God in many ways. We speak God's name with love and respect. We honor God.

We also show God our love when we worship God at Mass. Each week at Mass we remember God in a special way. We give thanks and praise to God for all he has done for us.

Thank You

Make a card to thank God for all he has done for you. Use words and pictures.

Faith Words

Great Commandment
The Great Commandment teaches us to love God, others, and ourselves.

The Great Commandment

God sent Jesus to show us how to live. In the New Testament we learn that Jesus taught us about the greatest commandment of all. This commandment is called the **Great Commandment.** Jesus taught,

> "Love God with all your heart. Love others as much as you love yourself."
>
> Based on Mark 12:29–31

The Great Commandment teaches us to love God, others, and ourselves.

How do you show your love for God, for other people, and for yourself?

What Does This Mean to Me?

The commandments help you to love God, other people, and yourself. You can show love in many ways.

Living God's Commandments

Put a smiling face next to the ways you can show your love for God, yourself, and others.

1. I can pray for others.
2. I can help out at home.
3. I can pay attention in school.
4. I can play fair on the playground.
5. I can share my toys with a friend.

My Faith Choice

Look at the chart above. Put a ✓ on what you will do this week to show your love.

And now we pray.

"Love your neighbor as yourself."

Matthew 22:39

Chapter Review

Circle the correct answer to finish each sentence.

1. A commandment is a _____ from God.

    law   **stoplight**

2. The _____ Commandments were given to us by God.

    Five   **Ten**

Write who the Great Commandment tells us to love.

_____

- -

_____

- -

_____

- -

_____

- -

_____

Think and share with your family.
Discuss ways you live the commandments with your family.

Visit our web site at
www.FaithFirst.com

We Love Others

20

We Pray

"Love one another as I have loved you. " Amen.

God helps us to love and care for others. What are some of the ways God wants us to show love for others?

We can show our love for others by the things we say and do each day.

Faith Focus

How does showing respect for others show God's love?

Showing Respect

"May I borrow your blue crayon?" "May I use your scissors?" It is important to ask before we borrow what belongs to someone else. When we do this, we show respect for them.

God's commandments ask us to respect others. Respecting others is a way to show love.

We can show respect by listening to one another. When we listen, we show that we care about the person speaking to us.

With My Family

Choose a member of your family. Surprise that person with special acts of love and kindness.

We also show respect when we are polite and kind to others. We can be helpful in all we say and do. We share God's love when we respect others.

Respecting Others

Look at the pictures on these pages. Now write or draw one way you can show respect.

We Respect What Belongs to Others

We take good care of what belongs to us. We also take good care of what belongs to others.

Respecting others also means respecting their belongings. We take care of what belongs to others. Taking care of what belongs to others shows respect for them.

There are many ways we can show respect for others' belongings. We ask before we borrow. We take good care of what we borrow. Then we return it and say, "Thank you."

Children in God's family care for and respect others. They care for and respect what belongs to others.

Respecting Property

You want to use your brother's new basketball. Write what you would say to him.

_____

- - - - - - - - - - - - - - - - - -

_____

- - - - - - - - - - - - - - - - - -

_____

Your friend asks to borrow your markers. Write what you would say.

_____

- - - - - - - - - - - - - - - - - -

_____

- - - - - - - - - - - - - - - - - -

_____

Telling the Truth

Truth is important. We need to be honest with our words and actions. It is important to tell the truth. When we tell the truth, people trust us.

Jesus always told the truth. We believe Jesus. We follow him. We show our love for Jesus and others when we live and speak the truth.

Imagine you are in the story. What would you say?

1.

2.

3.

4.

What Does This Mean to Me?

You follow God's commandments by respecting others and their belongings. You also tell the truth.

Showing Respect

Follow the directions in the story. For each blank, draw or write your story choice.

_____ is working with _____
Your name   Your friend's name

to make a _____ for their families.

They need crayons, paper, and _____ to make it. They are missing _____.

You ask _____ if you can please borrow
Your friend's name

the _____. When you are finished, you

return _____ and say, _____.

My Faith Choice

This week I will show respect for others and their belongings. I will remember to _____ _____.

And now we pray.
Show your wonderful love.
Psalm 17:7

Forgiving Others

Faith Focus

What is sin?

Faith Words

sin

Sin is choosing to do or say something we know is against God's laws.

"I love you." "Let me help you." "You are not my friend." "I do not like you." Words tell people how we feel. Sometimes we use words and actions to help others. We can also use words and actions to hurt others.

Making Choices

When we choose to hurt someone, we **sin.** Sin is choosing to do or say something against God's laws. Sin hurts our friendship with God and others.

When we sin, we turn away from God. After we sin, we often feel sorry for what we have done. Because we love God, we want to show God our love for him. We tell God we are sorry.

Words Can Help or Hurt

Circle the words that show love and kindness. Put an X on words that can hurt others.

Let's take turns.

You can go first.

You are my friend.

GO AWAY!

I'm sorry.

I forgive you.

It's my fault.

You started it!

I don't like you.

Leave me alone.

I won't play with you.

I can help you.

Asking for Forgiveness

We are following God's laws when we show love to others. When we choose to hurt others, we need to say we are sorry.

We need to say we are sorry to the persons we hurt. We also need to tell God we are sorry.

When we say we are sorry, we ask for forgiveness. We want to be forgiven! We want to make up. We want everything to be right again.

We also want God's forgiveness. God will always forgive us because God loves us.

A Forgiveness Prayer

Write a prayer to God asking for forgiveness.

With My Family

Think of and name ways you can say and show you are sorry. Think of and name ways you can show forgiveness to others.

God forgives us and asks us to forgive one another. If we hurt someone, we say we are sorry. We ask for forgiveness. We trust we will be forgiven.

Forgiving Others

It is not always easy to forgive others. When we might not want to forgive, God will always help us. When we forgive others, we open our hearts with love. We start over again and make a new beginning. Forgiveness is a sign of love. It shows our love for God and for one another.

How are the people in these pictures showing forgiveness?

What Does This Mean to Me?

You forgive others. When you forgive someone, it brings peace and love.

Forgiving Tree

In the leaves write words or actions that show forgiveness.

My Faith Choice

I will choose some of my forgiving words to say this week.

And now we pray.
Peace from God our Father.

Romans 1:7

Write the word for each definition.

1. This is choosing to hurt someone and God.

   S _____

2. This is what we say after we have hurt

   someone. I am S _____ .

3. This is what we ask for after we have hurt

   someone. F _____

Using pictures and words, draw and write
what forgiveness means to you.

Think and share with your family.

Make a forgiveness poster
with your family. Hang it up
to remind everyone about
forgiveness.

Jesus and the Children

A Scripture Story

22

We Pray

Come, children, listen to me.

Psalm 34:12

Jesus knows that children are very special. Jesus loves children. How do we show we love Jesus?

Jesus and the children.

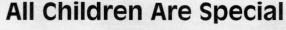

Bible Background

Faith Focus

What does the Bible tell us about Jesus?

All Children Are Special

Some children have big bright eyes. Others have a happy smile. Some are very quiet, while others talk all the time. All children are very different and very special. Jesus loves children very much.

Jesus was a loving person. He was God's own Son! Jesus taught the people about God our Father. The people understood what he told them.

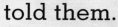

182

Jesus did amazing things! He made blind people see. He made crippled people walk. Everyone wanted to be with Jesus. The people wanted to touch him. They wanted their children to see Jesus.

Talking with Jesus

If you could sit next to Jesus, what would you talk about? Write or draw what you would tell Jesus.

Reading the Word of God

Jesus and the Children

A story from the Bible tells us that many children wanted to be with Jesus.

Parents had brought their children to him. They wanted Jesus to touch them. But Jesus was very, very tired.

People kept coming to see Jesus. All the people brought their children to see him.

The children came to see Jesus. But the disciples turned them away.

Jesus saw this. He stopped the disciples and he said, "Let the children come to me."

184

Then Jesus took the children. He hugged them. Jesus placed his hands on them and blessed them!

He said that they belonged to God. And God's kingdom belonged to them.

Based on Mark 10:13–16

Jesus loves all children!

With My Family

Act out the story of Jesus and the children. Make sure each person in your family has a part to play.

Drawing Me!

Draw yourself in the picture. Ask Jesus to bless you.

Faith Focus

What does Jesus do to show he loves the children?

God Our Father Cares For Us

In the Bible story, Jesus blessed the children. He showed them that he loves children in a special way. He calls all of the children to him. Jesus loves us too.

Jesus wants all people to be like the children. Jesus told us that the kingdom of God belongs to those who are like a child.

Children are cared for by adults. Children depend on their parents and other adults. They trust their parents' care.

How are the people in the pictures showing love and trust?

What Does This Mean to Me?

God, our heavenly Father, takes care of us. We can always trust that he will care for us.

Jesus loves you! You can show your love for Jesus by loving others.

Making an "I Care" Button

Use words and pictures to make an "I Care" button.

My Faith Choice

I will share Jesus' love with others this week by

_____ .

And now we pray.
"Let the children come to me."

Mark 10:14

Chapter Review

Circle the words in the puzzle.

Jesus	blesses	children	love

```
Q R T L B L E S S E S
Z W R B L L O V E A T
A B K C H I L D R E N
J E S U S M C S T R D
```

Use the words from the puzzle to tell how Jesus feels about children. Write your sentence.

_____

- -

_____

_____

- -

_____

_____

- -

_____

Think and share with your family.
Talk about ways your family loves and takes care of children. Thank your family for their love and care.

Visit our web site at
www.FaithFirst.com

Parent Page—Unit 4: We Pray

Your Role

Making a new friend or getting to know someone better is not always an easy thing for anybody to do, child or adult. As a first grader your child has probably made new friends this year. Perhaps you have also met some new people at your child's school, at your work, or in your church community. Whether that person moves from being a mere acquaintance to a true friend often depends on the amount of time and energy we put into getting to know that person better. Just as it takes time and energy to build human relationships, so it takes time and energy to build our relationship with God. Prayer is one very important way to build our relationship with God. Time spent in talking and listening to God can open us to new understandings of God's plan for our lives and to a deeper awareness of his great and never-failing love.

What We're Teaching

The fourth unit focuses on the importance of prayer in our lives. The children learn that we can talk to God in many ways. They are encouraged to pray anywhere and anytime. They learn the importance of praying throughout the day. They are encouraged to pray with their family at mealtime. The children will read the Scripture story of Jesus teaching his apostles to pray and learn the Lord's Prayer. You will want to review these chapters with your child and discuss the ways your family prays together.

Visit our web site at
www.FaithFirst.com

What Difference Does It Make?

In this age of communication, we are hardly ever out of touch. We have voice mail, E-mail, chat rooms, phones on planes, call waiting, cell phones, pagers, and beepers. There is constant communication. We work hard at making our communication better through technology because we know that communication is at the heart of all relationships. So it is with God.

Have you ever been so engrossed in doing something that you failed to hear someone speaking to you? You might have responded by saying, "I'm sorry. I just didn't hear you." In the midst of our busy days, we almost never have a moment of quiet to reflect on God, to sit and talk with him, or to just sit and listen to what he might be saying. Would spending more time in prayer make a difference in your life? Why not try and see if it does.

Unit Opener Photographs: (top left) stained-glass window of Jesus praying; (top right) boy appreciating God's creation; (bottom) girl praying in church.

We Talk to God

23

We open our
hearts and
our minds
to you in prayer!
Amen.

We talk to God
and others in
many ways.
Name some
ways you can
talk to God.

*We talk and
listen to God when
we pray.*

We Talk and Listen

We talk to each other in many ways. Sometimes we sing. We use sign language. We talk with our hands. A telephone and a computer help us to talk to someone who is not with us. Talking is a way of telling someone what is in our mind and in our heart.

We listen when others talk to us! Friends and families listen and talk to each other. Talking and listening help us to know one another.

Prayer is listening and talking to God. We tell God what is in our mind and in our heart. We can tell God anything!

We can talk to God anywhere and anytime.

Praying to God

We pray to God in many ways. Learn this sign language. Teach it to someone else.

I

talk

to

God

God Always Listens

We know God better when we talk to him. When we tell God all about ourselves, we get to know God and ourselves better.

We are part of God's family. Because he is our Father, God wants us to be close to him. He wants us to talk to him. God always listens to us!

_____

_____

_____

_____

_____

_____

_____

_____

_____

Jesus tells us it is important to pray. We are close to God when we pray. We can ask him to take care of us. We can ask God to help us to follow him. Talking and listening to God is important because it helps us to get to know God.

Telling God About Ourselves

We can talk to God about ourselves. Look at the pictures. Under each picture write a short prayer the child might be saying.

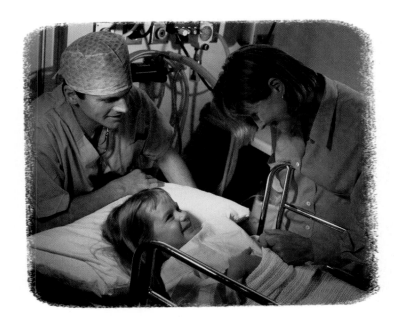

_____

_____

_____

_____

_____

_____

_____

_____

_____

With My Family

Begin your mealtime with a family prayer. Ask each family member to add their own words to the prayer. When everyone has had a turn, end the prayer with "Amen."

Jesus Shows Us How to Pray

Jesus shows us that God was the most important part of his life. Jesus prayed all through his life. Jesus listened when God talked to him.

Sometimes Jesus prayed alone. He often went to a mountain to pray. Sometimes Jesus prayed with others. He prayed with his friends.

Jesus asked God to help him. He asked God to help others. Jesus thanked and praised God. By doing this, Jesus shows us how to pray.

Sometimes we pray alone. Sometimes we pray with others. We pray with our church community. We tell God we are happy to be his children.

Where and when do you like to pray?

What Does This Mean to Me?

Prayer is talking and listening to God. You can pray to God as Jesus did.

Praying to God

You can talk to God about anything. Write your prayer here.

Dear God,

Thank you for

_____

- - - - - - - - - - - - - - - -

_____ .

Help

_____

- - - - - - - - - - - - - - - -

_____ .

Bless

_____

- - - - - - - - - - - - - - - -

_____ .

Amen.

My Faith Choice

This week I will pray to

God for _____ .

And now we pray.
May God bless us.
Psalm 67:8

197

Chapter Review

Fill in the missing words from the word bank.

talking	listening	pray	praying

1. Jesus tells us it is important to
   _____

   _____ .

2. When we pray, we are
   _____

   _____ and

   _____

   _____

   _____ to God.

3. When we spend time _____,
   we get to know God better.

Circle the correct answers.

1. We can talk to God about anything.   **Yes   No**
2. We can talk to God anywhere.   **Yes   No**
3. God listens to our prayers.   **Yes   No**
4. We can pray only by ourselves.   **Yes   No**

Think and share with your family.
Talk about ways your family
prays together.

Visit our web site at
www.FaithFirst.com

Jesus Taught His Followers to Pray

A Scripture Story

24

We Pray

Pray always and for everything. Give thanks in the name of Jesus to God the Father. Amen.

Sometimes we pray alone. Sometimes we pray with others. What are some prayers you say with others?

Jesus teaches us to pray.

Bible Background

Faith Focus

How do we pray like Jesus?

With My Family

Make different kinds of prayer cards. Share them with your family and friends.

We Pray

Sometimes we pray alone. We talk to God and tell him we love him.

Sometimes we pray with others. We say grace before meals with our families. Together we ask God to bless our food.

At Mass we pray with our church family. We praise and thank God. We ask him to give us what we need.

We pray in our religion classes. We join with our friends to ask God to help us to follow Jesus.

Jesus Prayed

Jesus prayed alone. He talked with his Father about everything.

Jesus prayed with others. He prayed with the little children who came to him. Jesus blessed them.

Jesus prayed with his friends. He even taught them to pray. Jesus teaches us about prayer.

Praying in Many Ways

Think of yourself praying with others. Draw a picture in the frame above.

Faith Focus

What does Jesus teach us about prayer?

Learning to Pray

In the Bible we learn what Jesus taught us about prayer. He told us to keep praying. He even helped us to understand how to pray.

One time Jesus was with his followers on a mountain. Jesus began to teach them about prayer.

Jesus told his followers to pray. He said, "When you pray, pray so others will not always see you. Go into a room and close the door. Then pray to God your Father."

"You do not need to use many words when you talk to God. Talk to God, using simple words from your heart."

Based on Matthew 6:6–7

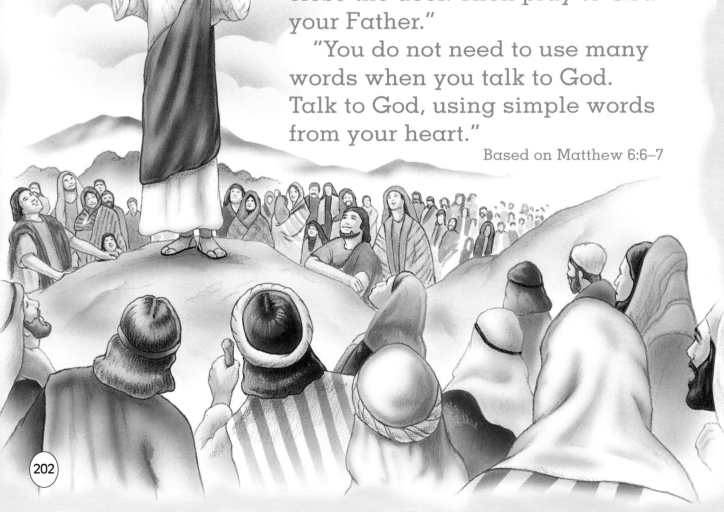

Jesus taught his followers to pray to God. God will listen and take care of us.

Learning to Pray

Find out what Jesus asks us to do every day. Use one color to color the spaces with an X. Use bright colors to fill in the other shapes.

God Hears Our Prayers

Jesus tells us to pray every day. Jesus wants us to pray to God our Father with our hearts.

Prayer is very important. When we talk with God, we need to use simple words. God will listen to us and answer.

Sometimes God's answer to our prayer is not what we think it should be. God answers our prayers in a way that is best for us and for others. Jesus asks us to trust God because he will always take care of us.

Have you ever prayed like these people in these pictures?

When you pray, you can pray as Jesus did. You can pray alone or with others.

Praying to God

Close your eyes. Think of yourself in your favorite place. Talk to God in your own words. Open your eyes.

Draw yourself in your favorite place. Write your prayer to God.

_____

- - - - - - - - - - - - - - - - - -

_____

My Faith Choice

This week try to remember to spend some time talking with God each day.

And now we pray.

To you I pray, O LORD.

Psalm 5:3

Chapter Review

Draw a line to connect the missing word to each sentence.

1. Jesus teaches us about _____ .   listen

2. Jesus prayed to his _____ .   prayer

3. God will _____ to our prayers.   Father

Decode a message about prayer.

A	B	C	D	E	F	G	H	I	J	K	L	M
1	2	3	4	5	6	7	8	9	10	11	12	13

N	O	P	Q	R	S	T	U	V	W	X	Y	Z
14	15	16	17	18	19	20	21	22	23	24	25	26

__ __ __ __ __ __ __ __ __
23 5   3 1 14   16 18 1 25

__ __ __ __ __ __ __ __
1 12 15 14 5   1 14 4

__ __ __ __ __ __ __ __ __ __ .
23 9 20 8   15 20 8 5 18 19

Think and share with your family.

What are some ways you and your family can show your trust in God?

Visit our web site at
www.FaithFirst.com

206

We Pray in Many Ways

25

We Pray

Sing a new song
to the Lord.
Amen.

Sometimes we
close our eyes to
pray. We use our
hands, our arms,
and our voices to
pray. How do
you pray?

*We can pray
anytime and
anywhere.*

207

We Pray

We use our voices and our bodies to help us to talk to others. Sometimes we talk to people with soft, quiet voices. Other times we might talk to people with loud, noisy voices.

We use our voices and bodies to tell people about ourselves. Together our voices and bodies can tell people how we feel.

We use our voices and bodies to talk to God. We can raise our voices in song, pray quietly, or just talk to God. When we talk to God with our voices or with our bodies, we are praying to God with our whole heart.

Praying with Actions

Finish writing this prayer. Then use actions as you pray the prayer out loud.

Dear God,

I pray to you with folded hands.

I pray to you with a quiet voice.

I pray to you with a smiling face.

I pray to tell you

_____

- -

_____

Prayer Actions

We use our bodies to help us to pray. We bow before the altar in church to show respect. Bowing is a sign that we love and honor God.

When we pray the Sign of the Cross, we use our right hand to bless ourselves. We say the prayer with our voice and with our hands.

In church we genuflect in the presence of Jesus. This means we touch our right knee to the floor.

Folding our hands also helps us to pray. We come to God as children with our hands held together. This shows our love and respect.

1. "In the name of the Father,

2. and of the Son,

3. & 4. and of the Holy Spirit

5. Amen."

Our actions help us to talk and listen to God. They also help us to show God our respect.

Prayer Actions

Look at each place where people pray. What prayer actions do you use in each place? Write the numbers beside each place.

Prayer Actions

1. genuflect

2. fold hands

3. bow head

4. hold hands

5. kneel

6. close eyes

in church

_____

_____

at meals

_____

_____

morning and night prayers

_____

_____

With My Family

Choose a song that you can sing to God. Make a book of actions to go with the song. Sing your song with the actions as your prayer to God.

Prayer Songs

One of the most beautiful ways we pray is by singing. When we sing our prayers, we use another gift God has given us. We praise God with our voices.

Singing our prayers means using words and music. We can sing alone or we can sing with others.

At Mass we sing with our church family. All of God's people join together and lift up their hearts to God in song.

Each of us has a favorite church song. These songs are called hymns.

What are some of your favorite hymns?

You can pray in many ways. You can use your arms, hands, body, and voice to praise God. You pray with your whole self.

Singing Songs to God

Sing this song to the tune of "Row, Row, Row Your Boat." Draw actions that you can do with the song.

Sing, sing, sing a song.
Sing a song to God.

Praise him. Praise him.
Praise him. Praise him.
Sing a prayer to God.

My Faith Choice

Pray to God this week by singing your new prayer song every day.

And now we pray.
"Rejoice and be glad."

Matthew 5:12

Chapter Review

Fill in the blanks to complete the sentences.

hymn	prayer	bless

1. Talking and listening to God is called

   _____

   _____ .

2. When we pray the Sign of the Cross, we use

   _____

   _____

   our right hand to _____ ourselves.

3. A prayer that we sing in church is called a

   _____

   _____ .

Draw a picture of a prayer action you like to use.

Think and share with your family.

Write a prayer-song with your family. Use it as a family prayer.

Visit our web site at
www.FaithFirst.com

Jesus Teaches Us to Pray

A Scripture Story

26

We Pray

Our Father
in heaven,
hallowed
is your name.
Based on Luke 11:2

Jesus taught us to pray. Many people have helped us to pray. Who helps you to pray?

We talk and listen to God.

Bible Background

Faith Focus

What does Jesus teach us about prayer?

Learning to Pray

Do you remember who first helped you to pray? Maybe it was a family member, a teacher, or someone at church.

Maybe they taught you to say good night to God before you went to bed. Maybe they helped you to learn the Sign of the Cross.

We are always learning how to pray. Our church family helps us.

Well, Jesus teaches us how to pray too! The Bible tells us that Jesus prayed all through his life. Jesus talked to God about everything and listened when God talked to him.

Jesus taught us that praying is important. Jesus also taught us that we should pray to God our Father.

Learning to Pray

In each picture frame, draw a picture of people who have helped you to pray. Write their names under their pictures.

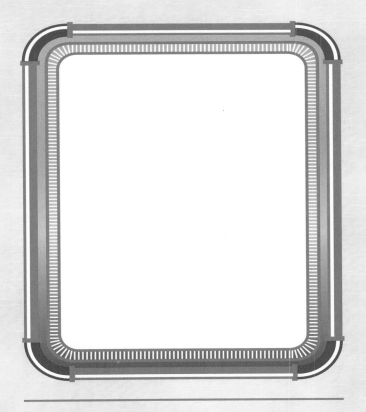

Reading the Word of God

Faith Focus

How did Jesus teach us to pray?

Faith Words

hallowed
The word hallowed means "holy."

Jesus Teaches Us to Pray

In the Bible we read that Jesus went up to a mountain to pray. The disciples of Jesus were with him. When Jesus finished praying, one of the disciples asked him to teach them to pray.

Jesus said, "When you pray, say, Father, hallowed is your name. Your kingdom come. Give us each day our daily bread. Forgive us our sins, as we forgive others. Help us to do good."

Based on Luke 11:1–4

We call this prayer the Our Father. Another name for this prayer is the Lord's Prayer. All Christians everywhere in the world pray this prayer.

Understanding the Our Father

Jesus gave us a special prayer for all God's people. Learn and say this rhyme about the Our Father.

Jesus taught us how to pray
the Our Father every day.

In this prayer we ask God's care
for each of us everywhere.

We ask for forgiveness for you
and me.
We ask for help to be the best we
can be.

In this prayer we give God praise
for all he does in all our days.

A Special Prayer

The Our Father is a prayer for all God's children. It is a prayer all Christians around the world say.

As we begin to pray, we say, "Our Father." We tell God that we believe he is our Father, and we honor his name.

When we pray the Our Father, we also show God our trust. We know that God cares for us, and God will give us what we need.

As God's children we ask for forgiveness. We forgive those who hurt us.

We ask God to help us to do good and to live together with God forever.

When do you pray the Our Father?

Faith Focus

How is the Our Father a prayer for all God's children?

With My Family

Hold hands together with your family and pray the Our Father.

You are a child of God.

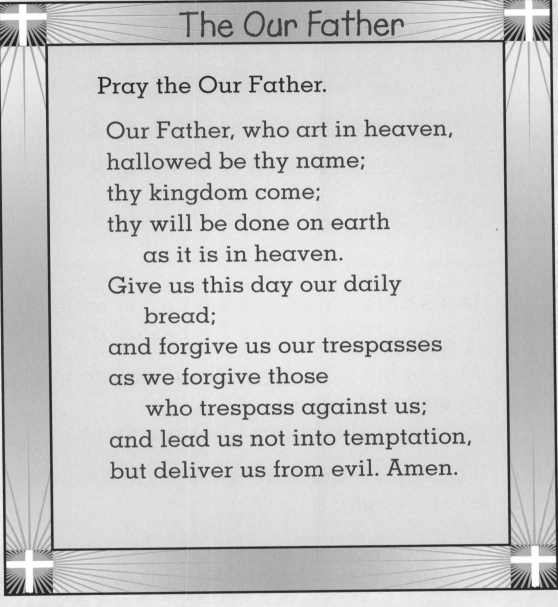

The Our Father

Pray the Our Father.

Our Father, who art in heaven,
hallowed be thy name;
thy kingdom come;
thy will be done on earth
    as it is in heaven.
Give us this day our daily
    bread;
and forgive us our trespasses
as we forgive those
    who trespass against us;
and lead us not into temptation,
but deliver us from evil. Amen.

My Faith Choice

Choose to live as a child of God this week. Say the Our Father each day and try to learn it by heart.

And now we pray.
"Lord, teach us to pray."

Luke 11:1

Chapter Review

Find and circle the words in the puzzle.

Jesus	Father	bread	forgive	prayer

J H O B R E A D W

F O R G I V E T P

M C J E S U S W Z

O P R A Y E R K H

L P R F A T H E R

Fill in the circle beside each correct answer.

1. Jesus taught us a special prayer called the _____ .
   ○ Our Father   ○ Glory Prayer

2. One of the _____ asked Jesus to teach them to pray.
   ○ daughters   ○ disciples

3. The Our Father teaches us that God is the _____ of all people.
   ○ Father   ○ brother

4. Another name for the Our Father is the _____ .
   ○ Sign of the Cross   ○ Lord's Prayer

Think and share with your family.

What are some ways and times you and your family can pray the Our Father together?

Visit our web site at
www.FaithFirst.com

We Celebrate
The Liturgical Seasons

Faith Focus

How do we celebrate our faith all year long?

We decorate our classrooms all year long. Decorations remind us of the seasons of the year—winter, spring, summer, and fall.

The Celebrations of Our Church

The Church has seasons too. We decorate our churches to celebrate these special times of the year. All year long we use different colors to help us celebrate. Purple or violet tells us it is Advent or Lent. We know we are celebrating Christmas or Easter when we see white or gold. At other times we see the priest wearing red or green.

The color we most often see is green. Green is the color for Ordinary Time, which is the longest time of the Church's year.

We Are Followers of Jesus

During Ordinary Time we listen to many stories about Jesus. In one of those stories, Jesus taught Peter about forgiving others. Write or draw how you might forgive others as Jesus asked us to do.

Faith Focus

How does celebrating Advent help us prepare for Christmas?

In winter the days seem shorter. We see less sunlight. We dream about the bright light of the summer sun.

Jesus Is Our Light

The Church's season of Advent comes at this time. During Advent we prepare for Christmas. We light candles to chase away the winter darkness. These candles remind us that Jesus is the light for our world.

Jesus asks us to be light for the world too. In Advent we let our light shine. We help people. We make gifts. We do secret good deeds for each other.

We gather in church and prepare our hearts to welcome Jesus. We sing and pray together. We remember that Jesus is with us every day.

My Light Shines

Decide what you can do to get ready for Christmas. Color in the flames to show what you will do.

I can pray.

I can help a neighbor.

I can make a gift.

I can help at home.

Faith Focus

Who are we waiting for during Advent?

Sometimes someone calls and announces, "Grandma is coming to visit you!" Then we get ourselves and our house ready for company.

Get Ready!

John the Baptist announced the coming of Jesus. People crowded around him. They asked, "How can we get ready?" He told them to make room in their hearts for Jesus.

Many people changed their ways. When Jesus came, they welcomed him with gladness.

During Advent we listen to John's message. We make room in our hearts for Jesus. We turn from selfish ways. When Christmas comes, we want to be ready to welcome Jesus.

Prepare to Welcome Jesus

Color in the boxes that show children preparing their hearts for Jesus.

Henry feeds his gerbils every day.

Abby pushes ahead of the others.

Tommy lets Angie ride his bike.

Patti will not do her chores.

Kanisha prays for her grandma.

Marie keeps all the candy.

Chris watches over baby Dominic.

Jack laughs at Billy's mistake.

Faith Focus

How does the story of Mary visiting Elizabeth help us to get ready for Christmas?

When we are happy, we sing for joy! We tell other people! Mary, the mother of Jesus, sang about her happiness. She also told someone.

Mary's Song

The angel Gabriel came to Mary to ask her to be Jesus' mother. She said she would do whatever God asked.

Then the angel told Mary that Elizabeth was going to have a baby too. Mary went to visit her.

Elizabeth saw Mary coming. She called Mary blessed because Mary said yes to God. Mary sang a prayer of praise and thanksgiving to God.

These gospel stories about Mary help us to get ready for Christmas. They teach us how to say yes to God.

Advent Prayer

Leader: Loving God, Christmas is almost here. Advent is almost over. Help us to say yes with Mary. Amen.

Reader: (Read Luke 1:26–33, 38.)

Leader: God called Mary to be the mother of Jesus.

All: And Mary said, Yes.

Leader: When God calls us,

All: We will say, Yes.

Leader: When God asks us to help one another,

All: We will say, Yes.

Leader: When God calls us to prayer,

All: We will say, Yes.

Leader: When God calls us today,

All: We will say, Yes.

Leader: Let us pray together.

Child 1: Hail Mary, full of grace. The Lord is with you.

Child 2: Blessed are you among women.

Child 3: Blessed is the fruit of your womb, Jesus.

All: Holy Mary, Mother of God, pray for us sinners, now and at the hour of our death. Amen.

The Fourth Week of Advent

Shepherds in the land where Jesus was born.

Faith Focus

During Advent who have we been preparing to welcome?

All Is Ready

During Advent we wait. Long ago, God's people waited too. They waited for the new leader God promised would be born. They wanted him to care for them. He would be a shepherd. He would care for them as a shepherd cares for his sheep.

The prophet Micah wrote that God's Promised One would be born in Bethlehem. Micah said, "He shall stand firm and shepherd his flock" (Micah 5:3).

The words of Micah came true. As Christmas draws near, we get ready to welcome Jesus our Savior who was born in Bethlehem. He is the Good Shepherd who watches over us.

Bethlehem

Follow the maze to help Mary and Joseph to find Bethlehem.

Faith Focus

Why did the angels visit the shepherds?

The Birth of Jesus

We like good news. It makes us happy. On the night of Jesus' birth, some shepherds heard good news. Angels said to them, "Today in the city of David a savior has been born for you" (Luke 2:11).

The shepherds hurried to Bethlehem where they found Jesus lying in a manger, just as the angels said. The shepherds were Jesus' first visitors. They told others all that happened.

We want to welcome Jesus just as the shepherds did. We thank God for bringing joy that will never end. We tell others this good news!

The First Week of Christmas

La Posadas

Mary and Joseph: In the name of God, can we stay here?

Innkeeper One: We have no room for you. We are too crowded!

Mary and Joseph: In the name of God, do you have room for us?

Innkeeper Two: We have no room here.

Mary and Joseph: In the name of God, do you have room for us?

Innkeeper Three: My inn is full. There is a stable in the hills. It is warm there against the chill.

Reader: (Read Luke 2:1–20.)

Leader: God our Father, we rejoice in the birth of your Son. May we always welcome him when he comes. May he be our joy now and forever. Amen.

Faith Focus

How can we continue our celebration of Christmas?

The Newborn King

During Advent we waited for Christmas. We waited to welcome Jesus, the Son of God.

On Christmas Day we listened to the angel's message: "Today in the city of David a savior has been born for you" (Luke 2:11). We know that this message is for everyone everywhere.

We now continue our celebration of Christmas. We want heaven and nature to sing and rejoice. We want the whole world to celebrate the birth of the newborn King. He is the Savior of the world.

We Celebrate the Birth of Jesus

Draw a picture that shows how you and your family celebrate Christmas.

The First Week of Lent

Faith Focus
How does celebrating Lent help us to get ready for Easter?

Think about spring. Remember how plants push their way up through the dark earth. Trees sprout leaves and buds. Birds sing their best songs.

Time to Grow

In spring we plant new seeds. We cut away dead twigs and stems. We prepare for new life.

Jesus talked about death and new life. He held up a seed and said,

> "Unless a grain of wheat falls to the ground and dies, it remains just a grain of wheat; but if it dies, it produces much fruit."
>
> John 12:24

During Lent we clear a place to
plant seeds of new faith and love.
We work and pray. We grow in love.

From Death to Life

Put this picture story in order.
Number each picture from 1 to 6.

Tell the story to a friend.

Praying Time

We like to talk to our friends. God is a friend who is always near. We talk to God in prayer and remember his love for us.

Jesus teaches us to pray every day. He says that God hears our prayer. God gives us all that is good for us.

Lent is a special time for prayer. It is a good time to offer praise and thanks. It is a good time to tell God our needs each and every day.

Lent is also a good time to join others in prayer. On Sunday we come together in our parish church. We praise and thank God together. We especially give thanks for Jesus.

My Prayer

In the spaces put words or pictures to complete your prayer.

Dear God,

I praise and thank you for

and .

I ask you to watch over

and .

Keep them in your care.

Amen.

Faith Focus

How does celebrating Lent help us to grow as followers of Jesus?

Better and Better

Making good choices helps us grow as children of God.

Once Jesus invited a tax collector to leave his work and follow him. The man's name was Matthew. He became one of Jesus' first disciples.

Jesus asks us to follow him too. During Lent we take special care to do the things Jesus asks us to do. We forgive. We find ways to make peace. We give to others who are in need.

We ask God to help us to make everything just a little bit better.

A Helping Prayer for Us All

After each verse, pray these words,
"Lord, every little bit helps."

When we can share
   by opening a door,
Lord, every little bit helps.

When we can help
   by sweeping the floor,
Lord, every little bit helps.

When we can add to the family fun,
Lord, every little bit helps.

When it won't work with just one,
Lord, every little bit helps.

When we need to pitch in to
   care for a pet,
Lord, every little bit helps.

When sharing is needed,
   don't let me forget,
Lord, every little bit helps.

Lord, help us today.

Amen.

The Fourth Week of Lent

Faith Focus

During Lent how can we be more generous?

Giving Our Time

We all like to help others. We like others to help us too.

Jesus asks us to help quietly. He tells us not to toot a loud horn so that everyone notices us doing good. Jesus says that only God needs to know our actions.

Jesus shows us many ways to give. We can visit people who are alone. We can feed people who are hungry.

Lent is a giving time. We give our time and share what we own. We help those who need our help. We work together to care for those in need. We pray for everyone who needs God's help and care.

We Share Our Time

We can help others as Jesus asked us. Write what you can do at different times of the day.

In the morning I can _____

_____ .

During the day I can _____

_____ .

After school I can _____

_____ .

At night I can _____

_____ .

Faith Focus

How can we grow as people who forgive others as God forgives us?

Has anyone ever said something that hurt you? Can you remember how hard it was to forgive?

Be at Peace

Jesus says that all his followers must be ready to forgive. They are not only to forgive someone one time but over and over again.

At Mass we forgive and ask for forgiveness. Together we pray, "Forgive us our trespasses as we forgive those who trespass against us." We are invited to share a greeting of peace with one another. The Church helps us to grow as people who forgive others.

During Lent we remember that God forgives us over and over. We try to become forgiving people.

Celebrate Forgiveness

Use this code to find out what Jesus asks you to do.

A	B	C	D	E	F	G	H	I	J	K	L	M
1	2	3	4	5	6	7	8	9	10	11	12	13

N	O	P	Q	R	S	T	U	V	W	X	Y	Z
14	15	16	17	18	19	20	21	22	23	24	25	26

__ __ __ __ __ __ __
6 15 18 7 9 22 5

__ __ __ __ __ __   __ __
15 20 8 5 18 19   1 19

__ __ __   __ __ __ __ __ __ __ __
7 15 4   6 15 18 7 9 22 5 19

__ __ __ .
25 15 21

Palm Sunday of the Lord's Passion

Faith Focus

How do we begin our celebration of Holy Week?

Welcoming Jesus

Sometimes important people come to our town or school. We go out and greet them. We cheer and rejoice!

Once Jesus came to the city of Jerusalem. He loved the people there. He wanted to gather them as a mother hen gathers her little chicks (Luke 13:34).

When Jesus came to the city, the people cheered. They waved branches from palm trees. They also spread their cloaks on the road to honor Jesus.

We remember this event at the beginning of Holy Week on Palm Sunday of the Lord's Passion. On this day we carry palm branches and honor Jesus too.

Honoring Jesus

Circle the words in the puzzle that tell about Palm Sunday.

```
T H O L Y W E E K E
P A L M S P C R L K
G J E R U S A L E M
L F M C L O A K B K
S E D M J E S U S T
```

Jesus and the disciples at the Last Supper.

Faith Focus

What does the Church celebrate on Holy Thursday?

Holy Thursday

Our Church celebrates special days. Holy Thursday is one of the most important days for our Church. On this day we remember and celebrate the day on which Jesus gave us the Eucharist.

On the night before he died, Jesus celebrated a special meal with his disciples. At that meal he took bread and said to them, "This is my body." He also took a cup of wine and said, "This is the cup of my blood." Then Jesus said to them, "Do this in memory of me."

We celebrate the Eucharist every time we celebrate Mass. When we do, we are doing what Jesus asked us to do.

Thank You, Jesus

Use the code to color the stained-glass window.

1 yellow

2 blue

3 purple

4 green

Triduum/Good Friday

Faith Focus

What does the Church celebrate on Good Friday?

Sometimes we look at pictures or a gift that someone has given us. This helps us to remember and think about that person. What do you look at to help you to remember someone?

Good Friday

The Friday of Holy Week is called Good Friday. It is a very special day for all Christians. It is the day on which Jesus suffered and died for us.

On Good Friday the deacon or priest holds up a cross for us to look at. Looking at the cross, we think about and remember how much Jesus loves us. One way we show our love for Jesus is by loving one another.

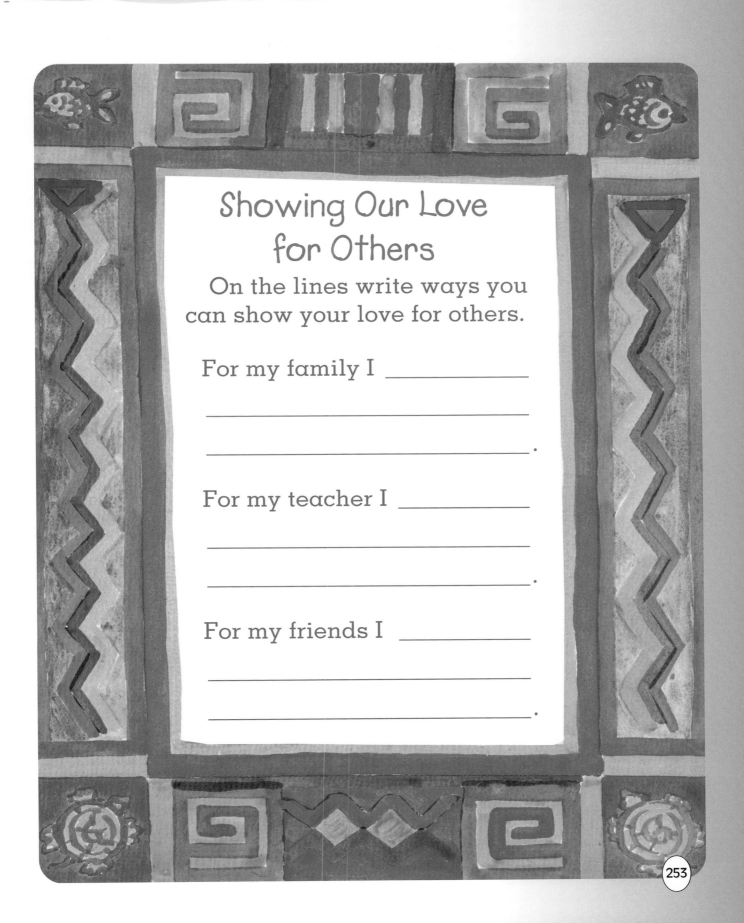

Showing Our Love for Others

On the lines write ways you can show your love for others.

For my family I _____

_____

_____.

For my teacher I _____

_____

_____.

For my friends I _____

_____

_____.

Easter People

At Easter we see signs of new life all around us. They remind us that Jesus was raised from the dead to new life. On Easter Sunday Christians celebrate Jesus' Resurrection.

We are Easter people! Alleluia is our song!

We sing Alleluia over and over during the fifty days of the Easter season. The word *Alleluia* means "Praise the Lord!" We praise God for raising Jesus from the dead to new life.

Every Sunday in the year is a little Easter. We sing. We rest. We enjoy one another. All year long we praise and thank God.

Praise the Lord

Decorate the Easter banner with color and words about new life.

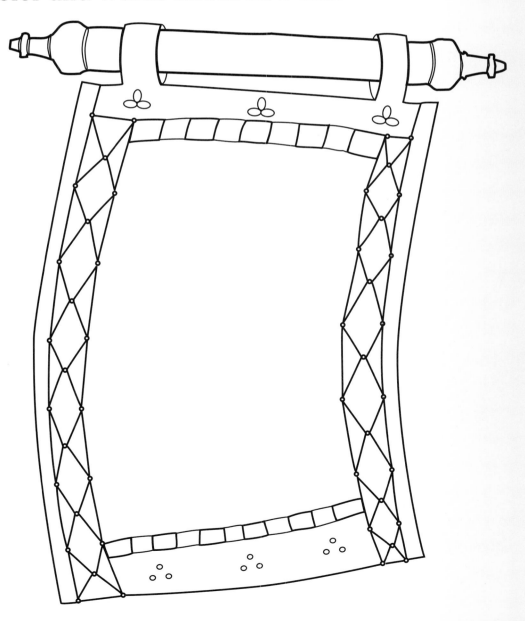

Telling Others About Jesus

We hear good news. Then we proclaim, or announce, it to others. During the Easter season we announce, "Christ is risen!"

For seven Sundays the Church joyfully tells Easter stories. We hear about the people who first saw the Risen Jesus.

Mary Magdalene saw Jesus and said, "I have seen the Lord" (John 20:18). Cleopas and another disciple knew the Risen Jesus in the breaking of the bread. When Thomas saw the Risen Jesus, he said, "My Lord and my God!" (John 20:28).

We too believe in the Risen Lord.
We show others that we believe in
Jesus by what we say and do.

Witnesses Today

Use your favorite colors to fill in the
squares that show the ways you can
be a good follower of Jesus.

I can help out around
the house. ☐

I can say my prayers each day. ☐

I can pay better attention
in school. ☐

I can play with someone who
has no one to play with. ☐

I can make a card to cheer
someone up. ☐

I can remember that God
always loves me. ☐

Faith Focus

What do we mean when we say that Jesus is the vine and we are the branches?

How do you feel when someone calls you their friend? One day Jesus called his disciples his friends. He said, "You are my friends" (John 15:14).

One with Jesus

This is how he talked about their friendship. He said,

"I am the vine, you are the branches."

John 15:5

He wanted them to know how special his friendship with them was. He was as close to them as a vine is to its branches. After Jesus died and was raised to new life, the disciples understood how much Jesus loved them. They knew how close they were to Jesus. They were one with him as a vine and its branches are one.

"I am the vine, you are the branches."

Jesus is one with us. He makes us one. At Easter we celebrate that we are one with the Risen Lord.

Alive in the Lord

Print your name on one branch. Print the names of other Christian people you know on the other branches.

Faith Focus

What did Jesus ask his disciples to do?

Proclaim the Resurrection

When someone loves us, we feel happy. Our smiling faces and actions tell people that we are lovable and loving and loved.

Out of love, God raised Jesus to new life. Jesus told his disciples to proclaim this good news to everyone. Then he returned to his Father. Out of love, Jesus sent his disciples the Holy Spirit.

Then the Holy Spirit came to the disciples. They were filled with joy and hope. They knew that God loved them. They told everyone the good news about Jesus.

The Spirit fills our hearts with joy too. Our words and actions tell others about the Risen Lord.

Every Sunday

Every Sunday we sing about Jesus' love for us. Trace the dots with a crayon to discover the missing word to the Church's song.

Christ has died.

Christ is risen.

Christ will come again.

Faith Focus

How did the early Christians show their love for one another?

The Growing Church

Each Sunday in the Easter season, we hear stories from the Acts of the Apostles. This book of the New Testament tells us about how people became followers of Jesus.

Jesus' followers loved one another as Jesus asked them to do. They offered food and clothing to people who needed them. They made sure everyone had a place to live. They prayed for one another. They took care of those who were sick. In all these ways they showed that they followed Jesus, who loved them.

Other people wanted to become Jesus' followers when they saw what the first Christians were doing. They wanted to do loving things too.

Following Jesus

Today our words and actions show that we follow the Risen Lord. Use the sentences and the words in the box to complete this puzzle.

Easter
Bible
prayed
followers
loved
Jesus

DOWN
1. Jesus loved his f ___ .
3. Jesus' followers l _____ one another.
4. We show that we love J____ by our words and actions.

ACROSS
2. The Acts of the Apostles is a book in the B____ .
5. During E____ we hear stories about how the Church grew.
6. The followers of Jesus p____ for one another.

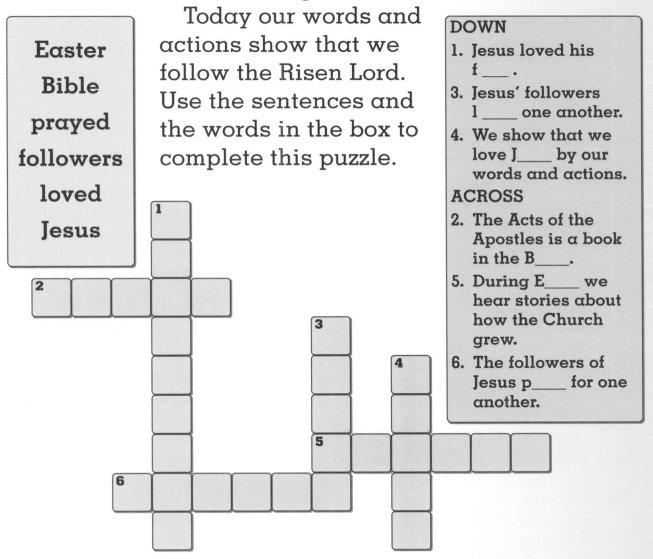

Write one way you can show your love for others.

_____

- -

_____

The Good Shepherd

Some of us have read stories about shepherds. Some of us have seen sheep on hillsides out in the country.

Jesus said, "I am the Good Shepherd."

At Mass during the Easter season we hear Jesus tell us that he is our good shepherd and we are his sheep. Once Jesus told Peter to lead the Church. He said to Peter,

"Feed my lambs" and "Feed my sheep."

John 21:15, 17

Jesus asked Peter to be a shepherd to all of us.

Jesus is our good shepherd. A good shepherd is willing to give his life for his sheep. During Easter we remember Jesus' love for us.

A Shepherd's Care

Read these Bible passages about
the work and care of the Good Shepherd.

The Lord is my ;

to safe

you lead me.

You guide me along the right  .

Based on Psalm 23:1, 2, 3

Like a

he feeds his  ;

in his arms he gathers the .

Based on Isaiah 40:11

There will be one  ,

one .

Based on John 10:16

Sometimes we leave home for a while to visit someone. Then we come back home. Jesus did this.

Jesus Returns to His Father

Forty days after Easter, Jesus led his disciples outside Jerusalem. He reminded them that he had suffered, died, and was raised to new life. Jesus said that they should share this good news with everyone.

Then he blessed them and returned to his Father in heaven.

The Church celebrates the day
Jesus returned to his Father. We
call this day the feast of the
Ascension.

Sing to High Heaven

Sing this song. Use the
melody from "Frère Jacques."

He is risen. He is risen.
Yes, he is. Yes, he is.
He will come in glory.
He will come in glory.
Yes, he will. Yes, he will.

Sound the trumpet.
Sound the trumpet.
He ascends. He ascends.
We await the Spirit.
We await the Spirit.
Yes, we do. Yes, we do.

We live by the Spirit.
We live by the Spirit.
Yes, we do. Yes, we do.
He will come and guide us.
He will come and help us.
Yes, he will. Yes, he will.

Pentecost

Faith Focus

When does the Holy Spirit help us to live as followers of Jesus?

Sometimes we receive a gift that we use to help others. We have received that kind of gift from Jesus.

The Gift of the Spirit

After Jesus returned to his Father, the disciples received the gift of the Holy Spirit. The Spirit helped them to share the good news about Jesus with others. He helped them to do good work in Jesus' name. The Holy Spirit helps us to do good. We do this in many ways. When we do good things in Jesus' name, we lead others to Jesus.

We celebrate Pentecost with great happiness. We have received the gift of the Holy Spirit.

The Gift of the Holy Spirit

Write your responses on the lines. Then say this prayer with your class.

Holy Spirit, help me to

_____

- -

_____

- -

_____ .

I praise you, God, for all you have given me.

Catholic Prayers and Practices

Sign of the Cross

In the name of the Father,
and of the Son,
and of the Holy Spirit. Amen.

Glory Prayer

Glory to the Father,
and to the Son,
and to the Holy Spirit:
as it was in the beginning, is now,
and will be for ever. Amen.

Prayer to the Holy Spirit

Come, Holy Spirit, fill the hearts
of your faithful.
And kindle in them the
fire of your love.
Send forth your Spirit and
they shall be created.
And you will renew the
face of the earth.

Lord's Prayer

Our Father, who art in heaven,
hallowed be thy name;
thy kingdom come;
thy will be done on earth
as it is in heaven.
Give us this day our daily bread;
and forgive us our trespasses
as we forgive those who trespass
against us;
and lead us not into temptation,
but deliver us from evil.
Amen.

Hail Mary

Hail Mary, full of grace,
the Lord is with you!
Blessed are you among women,
and blessed is the fruit
of your womb, Jesus.
Holy Mary, Mother of God,
pray for us sinners,
now and at the hour of our death.
Amen.

Act of Contrition

My God,
I am sorry for my sins
with all my heart.
In choosing to do wrong
and failing to do good,
I have sinned against you
whom I should love above all things.
I firmly intend, with your help,
to do penance,
to sin no more,
and to avoid whatever leads me to sin.
Our Savior Jesus Christ
suffered and died for us.
In his name, my God, have mercy.

Apostles' Creed

I believe in God,
   the Father almighty,
   creator of heaven and earth.

I believe in Jesus Christ,
   his only Son, our Lord.
   He was conceived by the power
      of the Holy Spirit
      and born of the Virgin Mary.
   He suffered under Pontius Pilate,
      was crucified, died, and was
      buried.
   He descended to the dead.

On the third day he rose again.
   He ascended into heaven,
   and is seated at the right hand
      of the Father.
   He will come again to judge
      the living and the dead.

I believe in the Holy Spirit,
   the holy catholic Church,
   the communion of saints,
   the forgiveness of sins,
   the resurrection of the body,
   and the life everlasting. Amen.

Nicene Creed

We believe in one God,
   the Father, the Almighty,
   maker of heaven and earth,
   of all that is seen and unseen.

We believe in one Lord, Jesus Christ,
   the only Son of God,
   eternally begotten of the Father,
   God from God, Light from Light,
   true God from true God,
   begotten, not made, one in Being
      with the Father.
   Through him all things were
      made.
   For us men and for our salvation
      he came down from heaven:

by the power of the Holy Spirit
   he was born of the Virgin Mary,
      and became man.

For our sake he was crucified under
      Pontius Pilate;
   he suffered, died, and was buried.
   On the third day he rose again
      in fulfillment of the Scriptures;

he ascended into heaven
   and is seated at the right hand
      of the Father.
He will come again in glory to judge
   the living and the dead,
   and his kingdom will have no end.

We believe in the Holy Spirit, the
      Lord, the giver of life,
   who proceeds from the Father
      and the Son.
   With the Father and the Son he is
      worshiped and glorified.
   He has spoken through the
      Prophets.
   We believe in one holy catholic
      and apostolic Church.
   We acknowledge one baptism for
      the forgiveness of sins.
   We look for the resurrection of the
      dead, and the life of the world
      to come.
   Amen.

Rosary

Catholics pray the rosary to honor Mary and remember the important events in the life of Jesus and Mary. There are fifteen mysteries of the rosary. The word *mystery* means "the wonderful things God has done for us."

We begin praying the rosary by praying the Apostles' Creed, the Lord's Prayer, and three Hail Marys. Each mystery of the rosary is prayed by praying the Lord's Prayer once, the Hail Mary ten times, and the Glory Prayer once. When we have finished the last mystery, we pray the Hail, Holy Queen.

Joyful Mysteries

1. The Annunciation
2. The Visitation
3. The Nativity
4. The Presentation
5. The Finding of Jesus in the Temple

Sorrowful Mysteries

6. The Agony in the Garden
7. The Scourging at the Pillar
8. The Crowning with Thorns
9. The Carrying of the Cross
10. The Crucifixion

Glorious Mysteries

11. The Resurrection
12. The Ascension
13. The Coming of the Holy Spirit
14. The Assumption of Mary
15. The Coronation of Mary

A Vocation Prayer

God, I know you will call me
for special work in my life.
Help me follow Jesus each day
and be ready to answer your call.

The Seven Sacraments

Sacraments of Initiation
   Baptism
   Confirmation
   Eucharist
Sacraments of Healing
   Reconciliation
   Anointing of the Sick
**Sacraments at the Service
 of Communion**
   Holy Orders
   Matrimony

Grace Before Meals

Bless us, O Lord,
   and these your gifts
which we are about to receive
   from your goodness.
Through Christ our Lord.
Amen.

Grace After Meals

We give you thanks for all your gifts,
   almighty God,
living and reigning now and for ever.
Amen.

The Great Commandment

"You shall love the Lord,
your God, with all your
heart, with all your soul,
and with all your mind. . . .
You shall love your neighbor as
yourself."

MATTHEW 22:37, 39

The Ten Commandments

1. I am the LORD your God: you shall not have strange gods before me.
2. You shall not take the name of the LORD your God in vain.
3. Remember to keep holy the LORD's Day.
4. Honor your father and your mother.
5. You shall not kill.
6. You shall not commit adultery.
7. You shall not steal.
8. You shall not bear false witness against your neighbor.
9. You shall not covet your neighbor's wife.
10. You shall not covet your neighbor's goods.

Celebrating Mass

Introductory Rites

**We remember that we are the community
of the Church. We prepare to listen to the Word of God
and to celebrate the Eucharist.**

Entrance Procession and Gathering Song

We stand as the priest-presider and other ministers enter the assembly. We sing a gathering song. The priest kisses the altar. He then goes to the chair where he presides over the celebration.

Greeting

The priest leads us in praying the Sign of the Cross together. The priest greets us, and we say, **"And also with you."**

Penitential Rite

We admit our wrongdoings. We bless God for his mercy.

Gloria

We praise God for all the good he has done for us.

Opening Prayer

The priest leads us in praying the Opening Prayer.
We respond, **"Amen."**

Liturgy of the Word

**God speaks to us today.
We listen and respond to God's Word.**

First Reading

We sit and listen as the reader reads from the Old Testament or from the Acts of the Apostles. The reader concludes, "The word of the Lord." We respond, **"Thanks be to God."**

Responsorial Psalm

The song leader leads us in singing a psalm. This helps us think about what we heard in the first reading.

Second Reading

The reader reads from the New Testament, but not from the four Gospels. The reader concludes, "The word of the Lord." We respond, **"Thanks be to God."**

Gospel Acclamation

We stand to honor Christ present with us in the Gospel. The song leader leads us in singing "Alleluia, Alleluia, Alleluia."

Gospel

The priest or deacon proclaims, "A reading from the holy gospel according to (name of gospel writer)." We respond, **"Glory to you, Lord."** He proclaims the gospel.

At the end, he says, "The gospel of the Lord."

We respond, **"Praise to you, Lord Jesus Christ."**

Homily

We sit and think about what God is saying to us. The priest or deacon helps the whole community to understand the Word of God spoken to us in the readings.

Profession of Faith

We stand and profess our faith. We pray the Nicene Creed together.

General Intercessions

The priest or deacon leads us in praying for our Church and its leaders, our country and its leaders, for ourselves and others, for the sick and those who have died. We can respond to each prayer in several ways. One way we respond is, **"Lord, hear our prayer."**

Liturgy of the Eucharist
We join with Jesus and the Holy Spirit to give thanks and praise to God the Father.

Preparation of the Altar and Gifts

We sit as the altar table is prepared and the collection is taken up. We share our blessings with the community of the Church and especially with those in need. The song leader may lead us in singing a song. The gifts of bread and wine are brought to the altar.

The priest lifts up the bread and blesses God for all our gifts. He prays, "Blessed are you, Lord, God of all creation."

We respond, **"Blessed be God for ever."**

The priest lifts up the cup of wine and blesses God for his blessings to us. He prays, "Blessed are you, Lord, God of all creation."

We respond, **"Blessed be God for ever."**

The priest invites us,
Pray, my brothers and sisters, that our sacrifice may be acceptable to God, the almighty Father.

We respond,
May the Lord accept the sacrifice at your hands for the praise and glory of his name, for our good, and the good of all his Church.

We stand and the priest leads us in praying the Prayer over the Gifts.

We respond, **"Amen."**

Eucharistic Prayer

Preface

The priest invites us to join in praying the Church's great prayer of praise and thanksgiving to God the Father.

Priest: The Lord be with you.

Assembly: And also with you.

Priest: Lift up your hearts.

Assembly: We lift them up to the Lord.

Priest: Let us give thanks to the Lord our God.

Assembly: It is right to give him thanks and praise.

Acclamation

After the priest sings the Preface, we join in acclaiming,

Holy, holy, holy Lord, God of power and might.
Heaven and earth are full of your glory.
Hosanna in the highest.
Blessed is he who comes in the name of the Lord.
Hosanna in the highest.

The priest leads the assembly in praying the eucharistic prayer. We call upon the Holy Spirit to make our gifts of bread and wine holy and that they become the Body and Blood of Jesus. We recall what happened at the Last Supper. The bread and wine become the Body and Blood of the Lord. Jesus is truly and really present under the appearances of bread and wine.

Memorial Acclamation

The priest or deacon sings, "Let us proclaim the mystery of faith":
We respond, **"Christ has died, Christ is risen, Christ will come again."**
The priest prays for the Church. He prays for the living and the dead.

Doxology

The priest concludes the eucharist prayer. He sings,

Through him, with him, in him, in the unity of the Holy Spirit, all glory and honor is yours, almighty Father, for ever and ever.

We respond by singing, **"Amen."**

Communion Rite

Lord's Prayer

We pray the Lord's Prayer together.

Sign of Peace

The priest invites us to share a sign of peace, saying, "The peace of the Lord be with you always."
We respond, **"And also with you."**
We share a sign of peace.

Breaking of the Bread

The priest breaks the host, the consecrated bread. We sing or say,

Lamb of God, you take away the sins of the world:
    have mercy on us.
Lamb of God, you take away the sins of the world:
    have mercy on us.
Lamb of God, you take away the sins of the world:
    grant us peace.

The priest raises the host and says,

This is the Lamb of God who takes away the sins of the world. Happy are those who are called to his supper.

We join with him and say,
Lord, I am not worthy to receive you, but only say the word and I shall be healed.
The priest receives Holy Communion. Next, members of the assembly receive Holy Communion. The priest or eucharistic minister holds up the host and says, "The body of Christ." We respond, **"Amen."** If we are to receive the Blood of Christ, the minister holds up the cup containing the consecrated wine and says, "The blood of Christ." We respond, **"Amen."**

Prayer After Communion
We stand as the priest invites us to pray, "Let us pray." He prays the Prayer After Communion. We respond, **"Amen."**

Concluding Rite
We are sent forth to do good works, praising and blessing the Lord.

Greeting
We stand. The priest greets us as we prepare to leave.
He says, "The Lord be with you."
We respond, **"And also with you."**

Blessing
The priest or deacon invites us,
Bow your heads and pray for God's blessing.
The priest blesses us in the name of the Holy Trinity.

May almighty God bless you, the Father, and the Son, and the Holy Spirit.
We respond, **"Amen."**

Dismissal
The priest or deacon says,
The Mass is ended, go in peace.
We respond, **"Thanks be to God."**

We sing a hymn.
The priest kisses the altar.
He and the other ministers leave in procession just as they entered.

The Sacrament of Reconciliation

Individual Rite of Reconciliation
Greeting
Scripture Reading
Confession of Sins
Act of Contrition
Absolution
Closing Prayer

Communal Rite of Reconciliation
Greeting
Scripture Reading
Homily
Examination of Conscience with Litany of Contrition and the Lord's Prayer
Individual Confession and Absolution
Closing Prayer

Glossary

Abraham

_____

- -

_____ was a
great leader of God's people.

Advent

_____

- -

_____ is the time of the
Church's year when we get ready for
Christmas.

angel

_____

- - - - - - - - - - - - - - - -

An _____ is a messenger
from God.

Annunciation

_____

- -

The _____
is the announcement of Jesus' birth to
Mary by the angel.

Ascension

_____

- -

The _____
of Jesus is his return to his Father after he
was raised from the dead.

Baptism

_____

- -

_____ is the sacrament in which we become members of the Church.

Bethlehem

_____

- -

_____ is the town where Jesus was born.

Bible

_____

- - - - - - - - - - - - - - - - - - -

The _____ is the written Word of God. It is the story of God's love for us.

Catholic

_____

- -

A _____ is a Christian who is a member of the Catholic Church.

Children of God

_____

- -

_____

love one another as Jesus taught us to do.

Christians

_____

- -

_____

believe in and follow Jesus.

Glossary

Christmas

_____ is
the time of the Church's year when we
remember and celebrate the birth of Jesus.

Church

The _____ is the
People of God.

Church's year

The _____
is made up of five seasons. They are
Advent, Christmas, Lent, Easter, and
Ordinary Time.

Creator

God is the _____ .
God made everything that is good.

Crucifixion

The _____
of Jesus means his being put on a cross
to die.

disciples   The followers of Jesus are called
_____

_____ .

Easter

_____

- -

_____ is the time of the Church's year when we celebrate that Jesus was raised from the dead.

Eucharist

_____

- -

The _____ is the sacrament in which we receive the Body and Blood of Christ.

Faith

_____

- -

_____ is trusting and believing in God.

God the Father

Jesus taught us to call God our loving

_____ _____ _____

- -

_____ _____ _____ .

gospel

_____

- -

The word _____ means "good news."

281

Glossary

Great Commandment

The _____

_____

teaches us to love God, others, and
ourselves.

hallowed

The word _____
means "holy."

Heaven

_____ is living with
God forever.

Holy Family

The _____
is Joseph, Mary, and Jesus.

Holy Spirit

The _____
is the helper Jesus promised would come
to help us.

Holy Trinity

_____ _____

The _____ _____
is one God in three Persons: God the
Father, God the Son, and God the Holy
Spirit.

Jerusalem

_____

_____ is
the city where Jesus taught and helped
people.

Jesus

_____

_____ is the Son of God
who became one of us.

Last Supper

_____ _____

The _____ _____
is the last meal Jesus ate with his
disciples before he died.

law

_____

A _____ is a rule that is good for
everyone.

Lent

_____

_____ is the time of the Church's
year when we remember Jesus' life and
death.

Glossary

Mary

_____

- - - - - - - - - - - - - - - -

_____ is the mother of Jesus, God's Son.

Mass

_____

- - - - - - - - - - - - - - - -

We gather at _____ to praise and thank God.

New Testament

_____ _____

- - - - - - - - - - - - - - - - - - - -

The _____ _____ is the second part of the Bible.

Old Testament

_____ _____

- - - - - - - - - - - - - - - - - - - -

The _____ _____ is the first part of the Bible.

Pentecost

_____

- - - - - - - - - - - - - - - - - - - -

_____ is the day the Holy Spirit came upon the disciples. It is the birthday of the Church.

People

_____

- - - - - - - - - - - - - - - -

_____ are God's creation. God created people in his image and likeness.

pray

_____

We _____ when we listen and talk to God.

Respect

_____

_____ is to care for someone and to treat that person as a child of God.

Resurrection

_____

The _____ of Jesus is his being raised from the dead.

sacraments

_____

The _____ are seven special celebrations of the Church. They celebrate that God is with us.

Saints

_____

_____ are holy people the Church honors. They now live with God forever in heaven.

Samaritan

_____

A _____ was someone from the land of Samaria.

Sea of Galilee _____

The _____
is the area where Jesus taught and helped
people.

Sin _____

- - - - - - - - - - - - - - -

_____ is choosing to do or say
something we know is against God's laws.

Son of God _____

- -

Jesus is the _____ .

Temple _____

- - - - - - - - - - - - - - - - - - - -

The _____ is the place
in Jerusalem where the Holy Family went
to worship God.

Ten Commandments
The laws God gave to Moses are called the

_____

- - - - - - - - - - - - -

_____

- -

_____ .

vocation _____

- -

A _____ is
God's call to live your life in a certain way.

Index